THE EARLY MANDOLIN

Embellishing Sixteenth-Century Music
Howard Mayer Brown

The Early Guitar
A History and Handbook
James Tyler

Editing Early Music
John Caldwell

A Treatise on the Fundamental Principles of Violin Playing
Leopold Mozart
Translated by Editha Knocker

Syntagma Musicum II
De Organographia Parts I and II
Michael Praetorius
Translated by David Z. Crookes

The Musical Guide
Parts I–III (1700–1721)
Friederich Erhardt Niedt
Translated by Pamela L. Poulin and Irmgard C. Taylor

The Early Mandolin
The Mandolino and the Neapolitan Mandoline
James Tyler and Paul Sparks

Play the Viol
The Complete Guide to Playing the Treble, Tenor, and Bass Viol
Alison Crum with Sonia Jackson

The Madrigal
Second Edition
Jerome Roche

Continuo Playing According to Handel
His Figured Bass Exercises with Commentary
David Ledbetter

The Baroque Clarinet
Albert R. Rice

The Art of the Trumpet-Maker
The Materials, Tools, and Techniques of the Seventeenth and Eighteenth
Centuries in Nuremberg
Robert Barclay

THE EARLY MANDOLIN

by

JAMES TYLER

AND

PAUL SPARKS

CLARENDON PRESS · OXFORD

Oxford University Press, Walton Street, Oxford OX2 6DP

Oxford New York Toronto
Delhi Bombay Calcutta Madras Karachi
Petaling Jaya Singapore Hong Kong Tokyo
Nairobi Dar es Salaam Cape Town
Melbourne Auckland
and associated companies in
Berlin Ibadan

Oxford is a trade mark of Oxford University Press

First published 1989
First published in paperback 1992

British Library Cataloguing in Publication Data
Tyler, James
The early mandolin: the mandolino and
the Neapolitan mandoline—
1. Mandolins to 1800
I. Title   II. Sparks, Paul
787'.65'90'

ISBN 0-19-318516-4 (hardback)
ISBN 0-19-8163029 (paperback)

Library of Congress Cataloging in Publication Data
Tyler, James.
The early mandolin | by James Tyler and Paul Sparks.
Bibliography: Includes index.
1. Mandolin.   I. Sparks, Paul.   II. Title.
ML1015.M2T9   1988   787'.65'09—dc19   88-18103

ISBN 0-19-318516-4 (hardback)
ISBN 0-19-8163029 (paperback)

Printed in Great Britain by
Butler & Tanner Ltd, Frome

PREFACE

UNTIL recently, very little research had been done into the historical background and repertory of the early mandolin. The possibility that there might have been *two* main types of early mandolin, each with its own design, tuning, playing technique, and musical history seems not to have been considered.

The earlier of the two types, gut-strung and played predominantly with the fingers, is still rarely regarded as a mandolin by modern writers, and the numerous surviving examples in collections throughout the world are often given misleading names, such as 'soprano lute' and 'mandora'. Even the examples made in the 1790s by the famous Presbler family have had their true identity obscured by the anachronistic label, 'pandurina', a term encountered only once historically (Praetorius, 1619) to describe an instrument from an earlier period, a different country, and with a different tuning and repertory.

Its repertory too, with only a few notable exceptions (such as Vivaldi's mandolin music), is largely unknown today, and the few notable exceptions have been wrongly assigned to the second of the two main types of mandolin, the one in most common use today, the later Neapolitan instrument, not yet developed in Vivaldi's time, designed for mostly metal strings, and played exclusively with a plectrum.

We shall call the earlier type of mandolin, the MANDOLINO, since this is the name most commonly used by its contemporary players, makers and composers; and we shall call the later type, the MANDOLINE, since, despite its southern Italian roots, its own considerable repertory was developed mainly in France.

It is important, given this negation in modern times of the mandolino as a mandolin, to define at the outset the precise nature of our two instruments.

In its classic seventeenth- and eighteenth-century form, the mandolino somewhat resembled a small lute. It had a small, pear-shaped outline with a rounded back; a completely flat soundboard with a decorative rosette, either carved into the same piece of wood, or constructed separately and inserted into the sound hole; and a lute-style bridge, glued on to the soundboard. Its four to six courses of double, or sometimes single, strings were of gut. It had a relatively wide neck, with eight or nine gut frets tied on; occasionally more frets of wood or another material were glued on to its soundboard. The soundboard was on the same plane as, or flush with, the fingerboard. Its peg-box was usually curved or sickle-shaped, with the pegs laterally inserted, but occasionally a flat pegboard, like that of a guitar, with the pegs inserted from the rear, is found.

The mandoline, developed in the mid-eighteenth century, also had a pear-shaped outline, but a much deeper, round-backed body. A distinctive new design feature was its bent or canted soundboard. Unlike the mandolino, it generally had an open sound hole, and its bridge was a thin, movable bar, over which the four courses of strings (almost always double), mostly or entirely of metal, passed from the tuning pegs to their point of attachment at the base of the instrument. Like the mandolino, the fingerboard of the early mandoline was flush with the soundboard. Typically, the mandoline had a flat, guitar-like pegboard, with the pegs inserted from the rear.

The mandolino's first five courses were tuned in fourths, and its sixth course a major third below the fifth course:

The mandoline's four courses were tuned in fifths throughout:

While the mandoline was plectrum-played from its inception in the mid-eighteenth century, the mandolino was played fingerstyle, like a lute, from the mid-seventeenth to the late eighteenth century when it too adopted the plectrum-style.

Having established the physical nature of the two early mandolins, we can now proceed to uncover the rich and varied musical history of these instruments (to *c*.1800) and the full extent of their respective repertories, which include works by Handel, Vivaldi, Sammartini, Alessandro Scarlatti, Hummel, Beethoven, and, as will become apparent from the source lists at the conclusion of Parts I and II, many others.

ACKNOWLEDGEMENTS

I WOULD like to express my sincere thanks to Robert Spencer and Maestro Marco Fornaciari for allowing me to examine the mandolino manuscripts in their private libraries; Avv. Giovanni Pellini for his help in locating the Fornaciari collection; the Curator of the Musikinstrumenten-Museum des Staatlichen Instituts für Musikforschung, Berlin for allowing me to reproduce photographs of its mandolinos; Dr Anthea Baird, Music Librarian at the University of London, for her help and co-operation during the research stage; Nigel North for the gift of a most valued microfilm from his collection; Manuel Morais for providing me with a copy of the world's only known Baroque bandurra music; Ugo Orlandi, and most especially, Stephen Morey, for bringing many manuscripts to my attention; Donald Gill for his help and advice; and, as always, my wife, Joyce for everything.

J.T.

September 1988

I am greatly indebted to the following people for their help and encouragement: in France, Christian Schneider and his family, and Françoise Granges and the staff of the Salle de Musique of the Bibliothèque Nationale, Paris; in the United States, Norman Levine; in Austria, Ulrike Greiner; in Denmark, Tove and Peter Flensborg and Kurt Jensen; in West Germany, Keith Harris; and in Great Britain, Richard Langham-Smith and Eric Clarke of The City University, who supervised my post-graduate research into mandolin history, and Jeremy Montagu of Oxford University. I would particularly like to thank Didier le Roux and Jean-Paul Bazin of Sartrouville, France, Stephen Morey of Sandringham, Australia, and Neil Gladd of the United States, all of whom have been independently researching into mandolin history and have given me great assistance prior to publication. Lastly, I would like to thank Hugo d'Alton of London for his endless enthusiasm and for his love of the mandolin which first inspired me to begin my research.

P.S.

September 1988

The publishers acknowledge the following with grateful thanks for permission to reproduce illustrations: Oxford University Press for Illustrations 1, 2, and 3; the Musée des arts decoratifs, Bordeaux for Illustration 5*a*; Sotheby's for Illustration 5*b*; and Euing Music Library, Glasgow for Illustration 15.

CONTENTS

LIST OF ILLUSTRATIONS

PART I

The Mandolino
by James Tyler

I

Origins

The Medieval Gittern

The small, pear-shaped, round-backed instrument, which was the ancestor of the mandolino, may have been known in medieval Europe from as early as the tenth century. Together with the 'ud' (developed later in Europe as the lute), the smaller instrument was one of the many introduced to Europe through western Islamic culture in Spain and southern Italy, legacies of the Arab world which have enriched our own.

Recent scholarship has shown that from at least the thirteenth century this instrument was known in Europe as the *quitaire*, *quinterne*, or *guisterne* in French; *gyterne* (later *gittern*) in English; *quinterne* in German; *guittarra* in Spanish; and *chitarra* or *chitarino* in Italian. It was not until well into the sixteenth century that these terms began to be applied to the various instruments which now comprise the early guitar family (Wright 1977 and 1984).

Although no specific music survives for the gittern (to use its English name), the instrument is very frequently seen in paintings and sculptures dating from the thirteenth to the sixteenth centuries. These visual sources suggest that the bowl-like body, neck, and peg-box were carved out of a single, solid block of wood. Over the bowl, a flat soundboard was glued with the rosette either carved into the soundboard, or constructed separately and inset. The bridge was either a glued-on string fastener, as on a lute, or, less commonly, a movable bridge with the strings running over it and attached at the base of the instrument. The peg-box was usually of the curved, sickle-shaped variety with laterally-fitted pegs. The number of strings could be three, four, or more (as single strings), or eight strings arranged in pairs to form four 'courses', or groups of strings. (The standard term, 'course', is used to mean each separate string unit, whether it be single, double or triple.) The strings were generally of gut, though some players may have used metal.

To my knowledge, only two instruments survive from this period. The

first is a tiny Italian example from the fourteenth century, which is now in
New York (Irwin Untermyer Collection), and is illustrated in Winternitz
(1966, 59). Its one-piece body, neck, and sickle-shaped peg-box are beautifully and elaborately carved, and there is a carved inset rosette of wood
(original?) in the soundboard. The pegs are missing, but there are five peg-
holes which might imply either five single strings or three courses (1 × 2 × 2).
The fingerboard and soundboard, both on the same plane, seem to have
been altered, so it is difficult to say what these details were like originally.
Winternitz refers to this instrument as a 'fidel', but it has every appearance
of a gittern, despite the unusual protrusion at the base. The peg-box is sur-
mounted by a carved female figure plucking a gittern.

The second surviving instrument from this period is by Hans Oth of
Nuremberg (*c*.1450). Now in Eisenbach, East Germany, it is illustrated and
described in detail by Hellwig (1974, 24–5). Again, the pear-shaped body,
neck and sickle-shaped peg-box are carved from one piece of wood. It has an
inset rosette of wood in a Gothic design which is quite elaborate, and ten
pegs for five pairs of strings. The fingerboard is flush with the soundboard.
The bridge, a modern replacement, is movable, and the strings are attached
to the base of the body. The vibrating string length is 34 cm.

As mentioned above, no music written specifically for the medieval
gittern survives, but there is much vocal and unspecified dance music from
this period which could be played appropriately on it. Before playing it
though, one must tune it, and unfortunately there is very little information
available about tuning. One fourteenth-century manuscript provides a bit of
help, but it is far from decisive. Christopher Page (1980) interprets the
manuscript's gittern tuning to be for a four-course instrument tuned in
fourths, and it is interesting to note that such a tuning became standard for
the classic Italian mandolino from the seventeenth to the twentieth centuries. From the manuscript, Page deduces the nominal tuning to be A, d, g, c′;
however, if taken literally, and following modern pitch conventions, this
tuning proves to be an octave too low for a typical small medieval gittern. As
for right-hand technique, the use of a plectrum or quill seems to have been
universal for the gittern in the Middle Ages, as it also was for the lute.

Chitar(r)ino was the Italian term for the medieval gittern, though Dante,
in the first decade of the fourteenth century, also refers to it as the *chitarra*
(Wright 1977, 10, 12, 17). It is perhaps worth noting again that not until the
middle of the sixteenth century did the term *chitarrino* come to be applied to

the little four-course guitar, nor the term *chitarra* to the guitar in general (Tyler 1980, 25–34; Tyler 1984, sec. 2).

Pre-sixteenth-century Italian documents provide some valuable insights into the music-making at various courts, especially Ferrara, beginning in the first quarter of the fifteenth century. Of particular interest are the documents mentioning the musicians themselves, such as Leonardo del Chitarino, employed at the court in 1424, and the Duke himself, Leonello d'Este, who is known to have played the chitarino from at least 1437 (Lockwood 1975, 118–19).

Also in Leonello's service was the most famous plucked-instrument player of the century, Pietro Bono (de Burzellis) (*c*.1417–97). Praised by princes and poets alike, he was known throughout his career as Pietro Bono del Chitarino and, although we cannot conclude categorically that the term *chitarino* in relation to Pietro Bono refers to the medieval gittern (he was also a renowned lute player), it does seem a strong possibility. Pietro was noted for his highly intricate embellishments of melodic lines over 'grounds' or structural 'tenors', played by a second musician (often a lute player known as a 'tenorista' (Lockwood 1975)). It could very well have been that he played these virtuoso treble lines on the little chitarino/gittern.

Renaissance Developments

Between the time of Pietro Bono's death (1497) and the late sixteenth century, we find a notable increase in the amount of documented information about our little instrument but, unfortunately, there was still no standardized term for it and, throughout the sixteenth and early seventeenth centuries, it continued to be called by a bewildering variety of names.

During this period, we do, however, find a growing distinction between our instrument and the other high-pitched instruments of the lute family. The latter, as far as is known, always had six or more courses tuned to the following intervals: a 4th, a 4th, a major 3rd, a 4th, a 4th (like the larger lutes). This, as we shall see, was neither the tuning nor the number of courses of our instrument in the sixteenth century, and even in the seventeenth century, when it began to acquire up to six courses, its standard tuning was never that of the lute. (See Chapter 5 for a discussion on the soprano lute.)

As far as the physical characteristics of the instrument during this period are concerned, sixteenth-century pictures and descriptions begin to indicate more and more frequently a lute-like construction of the round back; that is, a construction of separate curved staves to form the back, onto which is joined a separate neck and peg-box. Sebastian Virdung in *Musica getutscht* (Basel, 1511) and, similarly, Martin Agricola in *Musica instrumentalis deudsch* (Wittenberg, 1529, enlarged 1545) illustrate this construction of the 'quintern', whilst contrasting it with the larger lute (see Illustration 1). Other sources sometimes show the peg-box as straight and lute-like, joined at an angle to the neck. The number of courses, whether for double or single strings, is usually four until well into the seventeenth century.

One does still see indications of the older, hollowed-out construction in the sixteenth century, but this becomes more and more rare. One such indi-

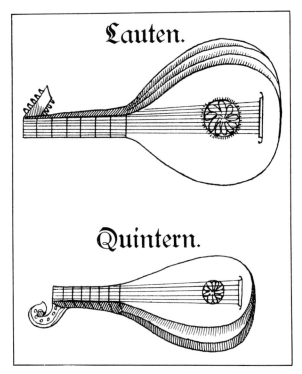

Illustration 1. Lute and mandore ('Quintern') from M. Agricola, *Musica Instrumentalis Deudsch* (1529).

cation of its continued use is the description by the Spaniard, Juan Bermudo, in his *Libro primo de la declaracion de instrumentos* (Ossuna, 1555). Bermudo describes the bandurria (libro secundo cap. xxxii and libro quarto cap. lxviii and lxix) as having three strings in the fashion of a rabel. He does not describe the shape or construction of the instrument; however, as the bandurria had the same stringing arrangement as the rabel, perhaps it also had the same shape and construction. Of course there is no firm evidence as to the shape of the sixteenth-century rabel, but in the seventeenth century, Sebastian de Covarrubias (*Tesoro de la lingua castellana*, 1611, fo. 119) defines the rabel as a three-stringed, bowed instrument, all of one piece and high-pitched, and the bandurria as being like a little rabel, all in one piece and hollowed out.

Bermudo also gives us the tuning of the bandurria. The three strings, he says, were tuned to the intervals, from highest to lowest, of a 5th and a 4th, or the opposite, a 4th and a 5th. (As we shall see, these intervals were also characteristic of the French mandore.) Bermudo further mentions that some players tuned in fifths, and that there were other bandurrias with four and five strings. He gives no pitch names, but does add that some players used frets while others did not, and that, because the instrument was so small, it was difficult to fret it so that it was well in tune. The Spanish sources, then, seem to be suggesting that the early bandurria was a small lute- or rebec-like instrument with fifth and fourth tunings.

The French Mandore

The first information about our instrument in France appears in a manuscript from *c*.1583–7 (F:Pn fonds fr. 9152, fo. 166). Here a four-course mandore is illustrated, as well as a tuning chart in French tablature giving the following intervals: from the first (highest) course downward, a 5th, a 4th, and a 5th. Specific pitches are not given. The illustration and tuning chart are reproduced in Gill (1985).

The first music known to have been written specifically for the instrument was Pierre Brunet's *Tablature de Mandorre*, published in Paris in 1578. Unfortunately, this book is now lost, as is the next known publication, Adrian Le Roy's *L'Instruction pour la mandorre* (Paris, 1585). Details of both these books can be found in Brown (1965) under the headings [1578$_2$] and

[1585₇]. It will have to be assumed that Brunet's and Le Roy's music required the interval tuning described in the Paris manuscript.

For the specific pitches to which the French mandore was tuned, we must turn to the earliest of the sources relating to this, Michael Praetorius's *Syntagma Musicum* (*tomus secundus*) of 1618–19. In a chart for the mandürichen on page 28, Praetorius gives the following three tunings, adding a fourth tuning on page 53:

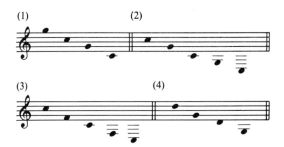

Note that tunings (1), (3), and (4) have the 5th, 4th, 5th intervals, and tuning (2), the 4th, 5th, 4th intervals, tuning combinations which both relate to those of Bermudo and the French manuscript. To my knowledge, the mandore (alias bandurria, alias mandürichen) is the only plucked instrument during this period to use these tuning combinations.

Praetorius gives the following further information about the instrument, as well as adding a few more names to our list of aliases:

Pandurina: Mandürichen. It is known by some as bandürichen, by others as mandoër or mandurinichen (because it is easy to handle and play). It is like a very little lute with four strings tuned thus: *g d′ g′ d″*. Some are also strung with five strings or courses and go easily under a cloak. It is used very much in France where some are so practised on them that they play courants, voltes, and other similar French dances and songs as well as passamezzi, fugues, and fantasias either with a feather quill as on the cittern or they can play with a single finger so rapidly, evenly, and purely as if three or four fingers were used. However, some use two or more fingers according to their own use. (p. 53; author's translation and italics.)

Praetorius then gives an actual illustration of the instrument (see Illustration 2, No. 5), calling it by yet another of its names, a mandörgen. Here it is a very small, round-backed instrument with four strings, a sickle-shaped peg-box, and a string length of exactly half that of the chorlaute (the standard

XVI

5

3

Z

1

6

4

1. Paduanische Theorba.   2. Laute mit Abzügen: oder Testudo Theorbata.   3. Chorlaute.
4. Quinterna.   5. Mandörgen.   6. Sechs Chörichte Chor Zitter;   7. Klein
Englisch Zitterlein.   8. Klein Geig/ Posche genant.

Illustration 2. Praetorius (1619), Plate XVI.

lute) (Illustration 2, No. 3).[1] Praetorius's standard lute has the first course tuned to g′, suggesting that his tuning (1) at g″ is the most appropriate for the mandörgen/mandore/mandoër/pandurina/mandurichen, etc.

The 5th, 4th, 5th tuning, as Praetorius implied, was particularly associated with France. As we shall see in the next chapter, this tuning was at variance with the Italian practice of tuning the little instrument (known in Italy during this period as the mandola), only in fourths.

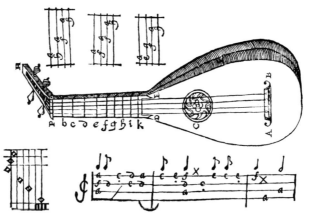

Illustration 3. Explanations of tuning and tablature for the mandore, with a passage from the second 'branle de Bocan' in Chancy's *Tablature de mandore*, from M. Mersenne, *Harmonie universelle* (Paris, 1636).

The French produced a considerable and highly distinctive repertory for the mandore (see Illustration 3), with surviving sources dating from *c*.1625 to the end of the seventeenth century. Music for the mandore also includes sources from Britain and from the German-speaking regions where the influence of French musical styles was strong. (An extensive survey of the French mandore and its music can be found in Tyler 1981*a*). Interest in writing for the mandore seems to have waned by the end of the seventeenth century, just as the Italian version of the instrument was about to enter its most active and exciting phase.

---

[1] Michael Praetorius, *Syntagma Musicum* (*tomus secundus*), (Wolfenbüttel, 1618–19; facs. edn., Kassell, 1958), plate 16; there is a modern translation of Parts I and II only by David Z. Crookes, which also includes the plates.

Surviving Instruments from the Renaissance

Several examples of the instrument under discussion survive from the latter part of the Renaissance. The first is by Magno Longo and is dated, Padua, 1599; it is found in the instrument collection of the Vienna Kunhistorisches Museum (no. C.38). It is a beautiful four-course instrument (the first single, the rest double) with a total string length of 23 cm(!). It is so small that one suspects it was made as a workshop test-piece rather than as a proper musical instrument to be played. Nevertheless, it is exact in every working detail. Another instrument from the same collection (no. C.41) is by Wendelin Tieffenbrucker (or Wendelio Venere, as there is some question as to the identity of this maker: see Harwood 1984). Dating from *c.*1600, it has four courses, the first single, the rest double, and a string length of 29.9 cm. Pohlmann (1975, 314) describes this instrument and Schlosser (1920, plate 6) includes a picture of it. Two further examples from the Vienna collection (nos. C.42 and C.43) are anonymous, probably Italian, and both finely made (Schlosser 1920). The first has four courses, the first single, the rest double; and the second has four single strings on a very narrow body shape. Another fine four-course example (the first single, the rest double), is in the instrument collection of the Music History Museum in Copenhagen (no. 300). It is a beautifully constructed instrument with ivory ribs and ivory facing on the neck and lute-type peg-box (Baines 1966, no. 199). Like the Vienna instruments, it appears to have been made in Italy and, therefore, should probably be called by the name by which it was known in Italy from the late sixteenth century, the mandola.

2

The Italian Mandola/Mandolino in the Seventeenth Century

The term *mandola* begins to appear in Italian documents from the late sixteenth century, first occurring in the descriptions of the famous Florentine *intermedi* of 1589.[1] Composed for performance between the acts of Girolamo Bargagli's comedy *La Pellegrina*, part of the festivities celebrating the wedding of Ferdinando I de' Medici and Christine of Lorraine, the *intermedi* required many voices and instruments, among the latter, a 'mandola'. According to the descriptions, a 'mandola' was used in Christoforo Malvezzi's sinfonia in the first *intermedio*, and in his madrigal, 'O qual risplende nube', in the sixth *intermedio* (Brown 1973, 109 and 128). As the mandola is only listed but is not assigned a specific line of music to play, we can only speculate as to how the instrument was employed.

In Agostino Agazzari's *Del sonare sopra'l basso* (Siena, 1607),[2] the 'pandora' (pp. 3–4) is included in a discussion of the use of such instruments as the lute, arpa doppia, cetera, lirone, and chitarrina.[3] Agazzari describes the pandora as a stringed instrument, not like the lute which has a full harmonic (chordal) capability, but like the violin which has little or none. He earlier mentions its use as an instrument for ornamentation that can decorate in a playful and contrapuntal manner. Agazzari's remarks suggest to me that the term 'pandora' was yet another name for our instrument.

---

[1] Wright (1977, 9) cites 1612 as the earliest instance.

[2] Facs. edn. Bologna, 1969; Eng. trans. in O. Strunk, *Source Readings in Music History* (London, 1952) 424–31. Agazzari's original reads: 'come ornamento sono quelli, che scherzando, e contrapontegiando, rendono più aggradevole, e sonora l'armonia; cioe Leuto, Tiorba, Arpa, Lirone, Cetera, Spinetto, Chitarrina, Violino, Pandora, et altri simili' (p. 1); and 'medesimente li stromenti di corde, alcuni contengono in loro perfetta armonia di parti, quale è l'Organo, Gravicembalo, Leuto, Arpadoppia etc: alcuni l'hanno imperfetta, quale è Cetera ordinaria, Lirone, Chitarrina; et altri poca, ò niente, come Viola, Violino, Pandora etc.' (p. 4).

[3] The term 'chitarrina', meaning the medieval gittern in earlier centuries, had come to mean the small four-course guitar by Agazzari's time. See Tyler 1980, 30–1.

The Italian lutenist, Alessandro Piccinini, in his *Intavolatura di liuto* (Bologna, 1623, reprinted Bologna, 1962 and Florence, 1984), tells us: 'In France they are used to playing a very small instrument of four single strings called the Mandolla, and they play it with the index finger alone. I have heard some players play very well ...'.[4] This description fits the French mandore perfectly, but the term 'Mandolla' is an Italian one which, to my knowledge, is not found in French sources. The French manner of playing the instrument with a single right-hand finger (with or without a plectrum tied to it), has been described by Tyler (1981*a*, 24, 26–7). One gets the impression from Piccinini's statement that in Italy (or, at least, in the Bologna region) the instrument was not yet as widely used as it was in France. It was, however, present in Italy, as the previous references to the mandola and certain surviving Italian instruments of the time attest.

One such instrument from Padua, dated 1630, is by an otherwise unknown maker with a highly dubious name, Catastro Parochiali (New York, Metropolitan Museum of Art, no. 1889). Its back is made of ivory ribs on which floral designs are engraved. It has five courses of double strings and a flat pegboard with the pegs inserted from the rear, in the manner of contemporary guitars. It has its original wooden case.

That a guitar-like pegboard was sometimes used on our instrument during this period is demonstrated by the extensive series of paintings by Evaristo Baschenis (1617–77) and his Bergamo studio assistants from the late 1630s to the 1670s. The instrument, seen from different angles and positions in the various pictures, has the flat, guitar-like pegboard with five courses (the first single and the rest double) in most of the paintings, though occasionally the same instrument is painted with a lute-style peg-box. The instrument depicted here is somewhat larger than most of the instruments we have been discussing, but is still smaller than the various lutes with which it appears in the paintings.[5]

Another surviving example (from *c*.1640) is the beautiful five-course instrument with sickle-shaped peg-box, made by Matteo Sellas, the outstanding lute and guitar maker (Leipzig, Musikinstrumenten-Museum der

---

[4] In Francia usano di suonare uno strumento piccolissimo da quattro corde semplici, e lo chiamano Mandolla, e lo suonano col deto indice solo, & ho udito suonare alcuni molto bene, & da questo stromento ho cavato il potersi ancora essercitare in tal modo di suonare in certe occasioni de gruppi tanto nel liuto, quanto nel Chitarrone.' (p. 7)

[5] For the complete series of paintings, see Rosci 1971.

Karl-Marx-Universität, no. 519).[6] It has the rather long string length of 37.5 centimetres.

Two instruments by Pietro Zenatto of Treviso should also be mentioned. One is dated 1651 (Washington, Smithsonian Collection no. 95, 259) and has a sickle-shaped peg-box with nine pegs arranged for five courses (the first single, the rest double), and ivory ribs. The other instrument is dated 1657 (The Hague, Gemeentemuseum). Also with ivory ribs and a sickle-shaped peg-box, this instrument is of interest for its early use of six double courses.

It is from the first half of the seventeenth century that we find the earliest use (to my knowledge) of the term *mandolino*. Amongst the papers of Cardinal Francesco Barbarini in Rome is a bill from an instrument maker dated 1634. The maker lists the following instruments which he has repaired for the Cardinal: '. . . la mandola e liuto e la lira e la tiorba . . .'. On the cover of the bill, the contents have been summarized by the Cardinal's secretary, who lists a case for the 'mandolini' (plural) (Hammond 1979, 105). This information implies separate meanings of the words mandola and mandolino, and suggests that the mandolino was perhaps the smaller of the two, hence the diminuitive ending '-ino'. This may have been the case in this instance, but, as we shall see, the mandola can often be shown to be the same size and have the same tuning as the instrument which others call the mandolino.

The earliest surviving source of Italian music for the instrument is from Florence during the reign of Ferdinando II de' Medici. It is in two small manuscripts, written in four-line Italian tablature, which are found in the Biblioteca Nazionale Centrale in Florence (I:Fn Magl. xix 28 and xix 29).[7] The instrument intended to play from these tablatures is not specified, but there are clues from which to draw a conclusion. On fo. 5 of I:Fn Magl. xix 28, for example, there is a scale chart:

[6] Described by Michael Saffle in 'Lutes and Related Instruments in Eight Important European and American Collections', *Journal of the Lute Society of America*, 9 (1976), pp. 48–9, 53.

[7] Described in Boetticher 1978, 107–8. They are incorrectly designated as guitar tablatures here, as they were in Tyler 1975, 341–7. This error is corrected in Tyler 1980, 146. See also Becherini 1959, 10–11.

This shows that the unnamed instrument is tuned:

To my knowledge, this is the earliest evidence of this tuning, which, with the addition of a fifth and, eventually, a sixth course, was to become the standard tuning for the mandola (later called the mandolino). This tuning has lasted into the twentieth century.

I:Fn Magl. xix 28 contains the following items in its twenty folios (bold type indicates the musical time-signature): fo. 1 ('Lucia'; fo. 1ᵛ–2 (untitled piece, 3); fo. 2ᵛ–3 'Pavaniglia in E';[8] fo. 3ᵛ (untitled piece, ¢); fo. 4 'Calata'; fo. 4ᵛ–5 'Gagliarda'; fo. 5 (the scale chart in staff notation and tablature); fo. 5ᵛ (another similar scale chart showing various sharpened and flattened notes and their position on the fingerboard); fo. 6 'Gagliarda figurata'; fo. 6ᵛ (blank four-line staves). The remaining fourteen folios contain blank staves.

The front paper cover of I:Fn Magl. xix 28 has the date 1670, but the repertory in this as well as in I:Fn Magl. xix 29 is more characteristic of the mid-seventeenth century. For example, the first piece, 'Lucia', is a series of fully written out chords to the popular song, 'Luciola viene a me', found in another Florence manuscript for voice and guitar of *c*.1625 (I:Fn Magl. xix 143, fo. 72) (Tyler 1980, 147; Becherini 1959, 68–9), as well as in other printed guitar books of the 1620s.

The written-out chords to 'Lucia' have stroke signs beneath the notes, similar to those found in guitar tablatures, which indicate that they are to be played using various down and up strokes with the right-hand fingers. I:Fn Magl. xix 29 supports this idea of strummed chords: on fo. 23ᵛ is a chart giving a guitar *alfabeto* (a shorthand system of chord symbols),[9] underneath which, in tablature, are the corresponding chords one would play on this instrument tuned in fourths. The *alfabeto* and stroke signs thus imply that the mandola/mandolino, in addition to its own repertory, might also make use of the huge guitar *alfabeto* repertory of solos, song accompaniments, and

---

[8] The 'E' refers to the 'key' of the piece in terms of the standard guitar *alfabeto* of the time. In this case, E represents what we would call today the key of D minor. See Tyler 1980, 66–7.

[9] For a detailed description of *alfabeto* and the strumming technique associated with it, see Tyler 1980, Ch. 5.

ensemble music.[10] The remaining pieces in ms. xix 28 are written in a predominantly single-line style interspersed with a few sparse chords.

I:Fn Magl. xix 29 contains the following items: fo. 1 'La Cocorocho'; fo.
1ᵛ–2 'Corrente'; fo. 2 [Bergamasca]; fo. 2ᵛ (untitled piece); fo. 3ʳ⁻ᵛ (blank);
fo. 4 'Ballo di Mantua'; fo. 4ᵛ–5 'Balletto'; fo. 5ᵛ–6ᵛ 'Ciaccone' (on fo. 6ᵛ is
written: 'ciaccone di . . . [unreadable]'); fo. 7 'Allemanda'; fo. 7ᵛ–8 'Balletto';
fo. 8ᵛ–9 'Passagli'; fo. 9ᵛ–10 'Toccata'; fo. 10ᵛ–12 'corrente' (fo. 11 'seguita la
corrente di la . . . [unreadable]'; fo. 11ᵛ 'seguito la corente di'; fo. 12 'Fine
della Corrente di Conti'); fo. 12ᵛ 'Balletto'; fo. 13 (untitled piece, 3); fo. 13ᵛ
'Corrente d.ᵃ la Fanta'; fo. 14 (untitled piece, 3); fo. 14ᵛ–15 'Ballo de
Cavalli'; fo. 15ᵛ 'Scappino'; fo. 16ʳ⁻ᵛ [ciaccone?]; fo. 17 (blank); fo. 17ᵛ
(untitled piece, c); fo. 18 (blank); fo. 18ᵛ (untitled series of arpeggios); fo. 19
'Pavaniglia'; fo. 19ᵛ–20 'Pavaniglia'; fo. 20ᵛ 'Bure di Monsu Agniolo'; fo. 21
(blank); fo. 21ᵛ (untitled, 3); fo. 22 (unreadable); fo. 22ᵛ (untitled series of
strummed chords followed by untitled piece); fo. 23 (untitled, 3 followed by
untitled, [3]); fo. 23ᵛ (*alfabeto* chord chart as mentioned above).

This manuscript is in the same hand as the previous one, and, except for
the piece on fo. 22ᵛ, all the items are in a single-line style with a few sparse
chords. An examination of the chords provides a clue to right-hand playing
technique: although nearly all the chords in the two manuscripts are laid out
on adjacent strings, which makes them easily playable with a plectrum, the
first two bars of the 'Scappino' (I:Fn Magl. xix 29, fo. 15ᵛ) contain a chord
with the first course open and, simultaneously, a note on the third course but
nothing on the intervening second. Although this could be a scribal error,
one must also consider the possibility that this music was played with the
fingers. As we shall see, this is definitely the case in later sources.

I:Fn Magl. xix 29 contains some clues which link it to the Florentine
court. For example, the 'Bure di Monsu Agniolo' (fo. 20ᵛ) (see Appendix II,
Example 1) and the 'Corrente di Conti' (fo. 10ᵛ–12) probably both refer to
Agnolo Conti, an important theorbo player at the Florentine court from
c.1631 to at least 1666 (Hammond 1974, 162). He is one of four plucked-
instrument players listed as being in the Capella and as being a composer;
the other three are Lorenzo Allegri, Pompeo da Modena, and Giovanni
Battista da Gagliano. The bass line to the 'Bure' is found in another Italian
manuscript, likely of Florentine provenance as well, which is a continuo

[10] For a comprehensive bibliography of original guitar sources, see Tyler 1980, appendices.

player's part book (F:Pn Rés. Vmc ms. 6). In this same Paris manuscript is also found the bass line to the 'Cocorocho' (fo. 12ᵛ), the same 'La Cocorocho' found in ms. I/Fn Magl. xix 29, fo. 1. It is probable that this piece refers to a *cocchiata*, a nocturnal serenade in a *cocchio* (coach), which became something of a custom in seventeenth-century Florence (*New Grove*, 'cocchiata'). It may be of interest that Conti's colleague in the Capella was Domenico Anglesi, who is known to have written a *cocchiata* in 1641 (*New Grove*, 'Anglesi, Domenico').

The 'Scappino' in I:Fn Magl. xix 29 is a *commedia dell'Arte* tune associated with the stock comic character by that name who, traditionally, was one of the most musical characters in a *commedia* company. The most famous 'Scappino' was Francesco Gabrielli (1588–*c*.1626), a member of the Confidenti troupe, whose patron was Don Giovanni de'Medici in Florence (Nicoll 1963, 172). Gabrielli was known for his great musical skill on many instruments including the guitar, the harp, and the mandola. One of his publications was the comic aria *Infermità, Testamento, e Morte di Francesco Gabrielli detto Scappino*, published in Verona in 1638, a twenty-eight stanza song with guitar *alfabeto*. In it, Gabrielli informs us that in his will he leaves his lute to the city of Ferrara, his violin to Cremona, his guitar to Venice, and his 'mandola' to Perugia (Pandolfi, 1957, 2: 11–17).

Important information regarding not only the construction of the instrument but, even more importantly, its name, comes down to us from no less a source than Antonio Stradivari. The great violin maker was also a maker of lutes, guitars, viols, and mandolins, and many of his detailed patterns and drawings for these instruments survive intact in the Museo Stradivariano, Cremona.[11] Written on some of the mandolin patterns, often in Stradivari's own hand, are the names and details of the various models of mandolin he built. All are of the type which modern museum collections incorrectly label 'pandurina' or 'soprano lute'. Stradivari calls each of them 'mandolino' or, for a larger-sized model, 'mandola'.

One of his paper outlines of a body and neck has the following inscription: 'Ant.º Stradivari Mandolino coristo' and 'Quest'é la forma del mandolino coristo' (no. 422). The total length from the top of the neck to the bottom of the body is 36.8 cm. The body alone is 25.2 cm, while the widest point across

---

[11] The collection is described and catalogued in Sacconi 1979; the mandolin material with photographs is found on pp. 18, 236–41. See also Frisoli 1971, 38–9.

is 11.6 cm. The neck is 4.1 cm wide at the nut and 4.5 cm at the lower end. The adjective 'coristo' probably indicates that it is the normal size for this type of instrument, a terminology similar to Praetorius's usage (p. 51) of 'Recht Chorist, oder Alt Laute' to designte the normal g′ lute. Other patterns for necks and sickle-shaped scrolls have just the term 'mandolino' and their model types inscribed on them.

Three of the body patterns are much larger than that of the 'mandolino coristo': no. 398, body length 46 cm and 20.6 cm wide; no. 399, length 40 cm × 20.4 cm; and no. 400, 35 cm × 23 cm. These are probably patterns for what Stradivari refers to as 'mandola' on various other neck patterns such as no. 403, 'mandola granda', and there is another measurement for a 'mandola piccola'. Stradivari, then, makes a size distinction in his terminology.

In all, Stradivari has seven different body patterns for mandolinos and three for mandolas. Further details include the nut and bridge string spacings (nos. 420 and 421), and one pattern which includes a flat, guitar-like pegboard (no. 419). The various peg-box patterns show the number and positions of the pegs (nos. 407 and 410: 8 pegs; no. 411: 9 pegs; no. 404: 10 pegs). Fret positions are shown as well.

Stradivari has left us a wealth of valuable information on the mandolino of the late seventeenth century, and, happily, two actual mandolinos by Stradivari survive as well. The first (Chichester, Christopher Challen Collection) is a five-course (all double) instrument, with a beautiful seven-ribbed maple back, sickle-shaped peg-box, and an inset rosette. The string length is 31.5 centimetres and inside, written in ink directly onto the wood, is the following: 'Antonio Stradivari in Cremona 1680'. The instrument is pictured in Tyler (1981*b*, 440). It has its original wooden case. The body corresponds most closely to Stradivari's pattern no. 423.

The second surviving Stradivari mandolino (London, Charles Beare Collection) has a nine-ribbed maple back and a rosette carved into the wood of the soundboard. It has nine pegs for five courses, the first being single, but there is evidence that the sickle-shaped peg-box originally had only eight pegs, the highest peg-hole having been drilled at a later date. Its classic simplicity is a delight to the eye.[12] This instrument corresponds to Stradivari's body pattern no. 419. Though there is no label, all the evidence points to its being a Stradivari mandolino dating from *c*.1706.

---

[12] The instrument is drawn and studied for its proportions in Coates 1985, 132–5. Another anonymous Italian mandolino, *c*.1640, is examined on pp. 128–31 of the same work.

The first printed music specifically for the small mandola appears in a guitar source, Giovanni Pietro Ricci's *Scuola d'intavolatura . . .* (Rome, 1677) (Tyler 1980, 132). Near the end of the book (pp. 50–3) is found a separate title-page which reads 'Sonate nuove di mandola . . .', followed by music which is headed 'Balletto allegro per la Mandola, del Sig. D. Gasparo Cantarelli Bolognese'. Another balletto follows. The music is in staff notation using the treble clef, with a range from g′ to b″. If these notes are to be played comfortably at their literal pitches on an instrument tuned to, say, the pitches of the Florence manuscripts previously discussed, then Cantarelli's mandola has to be rather more like the instrument Stradivari calls a mandolino than the larger one he calls a mandola. The music is entirely single-line, with no chords and no right- or left-hand markings, therefore we cannot be certain whether it is meant to be played with the right-hand fingers or with a plectrum.

Gasparo Cantarelli was a 'violone' player at the church of San Marcello in Rome from *c*.1663 to *c*.1685. In the 1660s, the Maestro di Capella was the renowned composer, lutenist, and guitarist, Lelio Colista, who directed the singers and instrumental ensemble and played continuo on lute and theorbo. A document survives from the year 1667 which lists the personnel for an oratorio performed at the church, including Cantarelli and Domenico(?) Melari della Mandola. Later payment documents also list Melari as a mandola player (Wesseley-Kropik 1961, 61, 81), and he seems to have been consistently employed as such at San Marcello, where he is listed as a player in another oratorio in 1668 and again in 1674, playing mandola with a second mandolist called 'Quintavalle'. Antonio Quintavale, *fl*.1674–1724, became the Maestro di Capella at San Marcello in 1694, and is also known to have composed oratorios and operas (Wesseley-Kropik 1961, 61; Liess 1957, 144, 146, 153, 166; *New Grove* 15: 510).

A manuscript of *c*.1675–85 is in the Conservatory in Florence (I:Fc 3802). On fo. 1 is written, presumably in a contemporary hand, 'Diverse arie di danza per mandola' and 'regola per accordare l'arpa'. The first twelve folios are for the mandola in four-line Italian tablature, and the remaining eighteen are for the harp in its own special tablature. All the music is anonymous. The mandola portion contains the following pieces: fo. 1–2ᵛ (blank); fo. 3 'Corrente' (see Appendix II, Example 2); fo. 3ᵛ 'Minuet'; fo. 4 'Ballo di Mantova'; fo. 4ᵛ–5 'Saltarello'; fo. 5ᵛ–6 'Corrente'; fo. 6ᵛ 'Minuet'; fo. 7 'Corrente'; fo. 7ᵛ 'Minuet'; fo. 8 'Borè'; fo. 8ᵛ–9 'Saltarello'; fo. 9 'Minuet';

fo. 9ᵛ 'Borè'; fo. 10–11 'Corrente'; fo. 11ᵛ–12 'Ballo di Mantova'; fo. 12 'Veneziana'; fo. 12ᵛ (scraps of staff notation); fo. 13 (scale chart showing notes in treble clef, the names of the strings on which they are found, and the numbers of the frets at which each note is found).

The scale chart shows the tuning to be the same as for the previous two Florentine manuscripts: g″ ('Cantino'), d″ ('Sottana'), a′ ('Mezzana'), e′ ('Bordone'). The music is in single-line style with occasional sparse chords. An examination of the chords indicates that several of the configurations are not on consecutive courses, and therefore a right-hand finger-style technique is required.

All the anonymous dance pieces in this manuscript are clearly notated and fun to play. I have found no concordances for any of them to date, except, of course, for the internationally known 'Ballo di Mantova', which is found in innumerable other versions.[13]

Another seventeenth-century mention of the term mandolino is found in Tomaso Motta's *Armonica capricciosa di suonate musicali* (Milan, 1681) (Sartori 1952, 499). On the title-page of this collection of his two-part instrumental music (for unspecified treble and bass instruments), Motta describes himself as a dancing master and a player of the Spanish guitar, lute, violin, and bass viol ('violone'). In his preface to the reader, he says that if his first publication is well received, there is a lot more music where that came from, including solo and ensemble music for 'arcileuto all'Italiana', 'Chitarra alla Spagnola', and 'Mandolino di quattro, ò cinque ò sei corde' (mandolin of four or five or six courses). Apparently Motta's book was not well received, for there is no evidence of any further publications. This, and the surviving Pietro Zenatto instrument of 1657, previously mentioned, are the earliest references I have found to a six-course mandolino.

In the library of Robert Spencer (London) is a manuscript of mostly guitar music with the inscription, 'questo libro e di Domenico Veterani' (fo. 29), and, following one of the pieces, the date, 1698 (fo. 23) (Tyler 1980, 145). The guitar pieces are primarily in the *alfabeto* style, with some pieces in mixed tablature (Tyler 1980, 74–6). The repertory consists of popular airs and dances consistent with the period between *c*.1650 and the 1690s. In addition to the guitar music, there is one piece in normal six-line Italian tablature for a lute of at least ten courses, and a series of pieces in five-line

---

[13] For a description of the tune and select concordances, see Tyler ed. 1983, vol. ii, pp. viii–ix.

tablature for an instrument requiring no more than five courses, but whose tuning intervals are not that of a guitar. These pieces require a tuning in fourths throughout. The instrument for which these pieces were written is not named in the manuscript, but I know of no plucked instrument of the time which used complete fourths except the mandola/mandolino. This identification is supported by the fact that these pieces, unlike the rest of the manuscript, are written primarily in single-line style, with a few sparse chords: exactly the same style of the other mandola/mandolino manuscripts previously discussed.

The mandola/mandolino pieces in the Veterani manuscript are as follows: fo. 9^{r-v} 'Ciachona'; fo. 10 'Saltarello'; fo. 10^v 'Minuetto'; fo. 11 'Sarabanda'; fo. 11^v 'La Bore francese'; fo. 12 'Tochata'. These simple but effective dance pieces, and the arpeggiated 'Tochata', have chord configurations which, once again, require a right-hand technique using the fingers rather than a plectrum.

According to the mandola/mandolino sources so far discussed, finger-style playing, that is, playing in the manner of the lute, seems to have been the norm in Italy during the seventeenth century. This suggests that the mandola/mandolino would have been a natural and convenient instrument for lute players to have used as an instrument on which to 'double' and there is much evidence for this having been the practice from the end of the seventeenth century. From the second half of the century, the lute was used increasingly in Italy in orchestras and ensembles for oratorios, operas, cantatas, and chamber music, and it is precisely in those performing circumstances that we find an increasing use of the mandola/mandolino later in the century.[14] For example, the lute and mandola were in the orchestra for the oratorio *Ismaele* by Carlo Cesarini in 1695 at San Marcello, Rome (Marx 1983, 163); two arias from the late seventeenth century survive from theatrical works by Giovanni Pietro Franchi, scored for four voices, violin, lute, and mandolino (*New Grove* 6: 774); and a cantata scored for two voices, two violins, cello, contrabasso, trumpet, mandola, and unspecified continuo

---

[14] See the numerous documents listing orchestra personnel cited in Marx (1983), Liess (1957), Gambassi (1984), Hammond (1974), Bowman (1981), Marx (1968). A history of the Italian baroque lute has yet to be written. The importance of the lute in Italy from *c.*1650 to the early years of the nineteenth century has been totally ignored, for example, in the most recent general history of the lute in *New Grove Dictionary of Musical Instruments*, (1984).

(perhaps lute), dated 1699, survives by one of the greatest and most influential of the baroque composers, Alessandro Scarlatti (*New Grove* 16: 562).

With the name Scarlatti, we arrive on the threshold of the eighteenth century, from which time there is a marked increase in the use of the mandolino by important composers, and the instrument enters what might be called a veritable golden age.

3

The Mandola/Mandolino in the Eighteenth Century

Throughout much of the eighteenth century, the terms mandola and man-dolino were interchangeable, always referring to the small, high-pitched instrument tuned in fourths. Our study of the instrument in the eighteenth century begins with an examination of a highly interesting manuscript found in Paris (F:Pn Rés Vmb ms. 9) entitled 'Libro per la Mandola dell Illuss.^{mo} Sig.^{re} Matteo Caccini a di p.^{o} Agosto 1703'. Nothing is known about Caccini (who was the owner/compiler of the manuscript rather than the composer of its music), but his famous surname suggests a connection with the family of Florentine musicians and composers of the same name. The designation, 'most illustrious Signor', indicates that he was a person of some social prominence, and Matteo could well have been related to Domenico Caccini, who was of minor nobility but influential at the Medici court (see Weaver 1978, 46, 141).

The manuscript is a thirty-six folio miscellany of short dances and prelude-like pieces. All the music is in staff notation using the treble clef. The first sixteen and the final two pieces are for mandola. These are in the single-line style with some chords in configurations consistent with those in the mandola/mandolino manuscripts discussed in the previous chapter. A scale chart on fo. 16^{v} gives the following (by now standard) mandola/mandolino tuning in fourths: g″ ('cantino'), d″ ('sotana'), a′ ('mezzana'), and e′ ('cordone') for a four-course instrument. The untitled exercise on fo. 3 shows, unequivocally, that the mandola is to be played finger-style; the right-hand fingerings are shown, as in lute music, with dots next to the respective notes; that is, one dot next to a note means the right-hand index finger is used, and two dots mean the middle finger is used:

The pieces for mandola are the following: fo. 1 'Minuet' and 'Buré'; fo. 1ᵛ 'Aria di Venezzia' and 'Aria'; fo. 2 'Minuet'; fo. 2ᵛ 'Saltarello di Meccoli'; fo. 3 'Aria di Venezzia' (and untitled arpeggio exercise shown above) and 'Passagio'; fo. 3ᵛ (untitled piece) 'di sig:re P. P. Cappelini'; fo. 4 (untitled piece) 'di sig:re P. P. Cappelini'; fo. 4ᵛ 'Alemanda di P. P. C.'; fo. 5 'Alemanda di Niccolò Ceccherini'; fos. 5ᵛ–6 'Fuga di Niccolò Ceccherini' (facsimile in Tyler 1981*b*, 442; see Appendix II, Example 3 for the 'Alemanda' and the 'Fuga'); fos. 6ᵛ–7 'Fuga'; fo. 7 'Giga'; fo. 36ᵛ 'Aria di Venezzia' and 'Alemanda'.

As regards the three composers identified in six of the pieces, Ceccherini is described elsewhere as having been a theorbist and chamber musician to the 'Serenissimo Gran Principe di Toscana' (presumably Cosimo III de' Medici),[1] and Pietro Paolo Cappelini was also a theorbist and a cantata composer, who was known to have been in the service of Pope Alexander VII in Rome in the mid-seventeenth century and who also accompanied Cardinal Flavio Chigi on a mission to Paris in 1664. On the same mission was Cappelini's colleague, Lelio Colista (Silbiger 1980, 119, 200; *New Grove* 3: 756). Meccoli is probably the same Federico Meccoli who, with Cappelini, Stradella, Pasquini, Cavalli, Cesti, and others, is represented in a Bolognese manuscript collection of cantatas,[2] and whose name is also found in the Paris continuo part-book referred to in Chapter 2 (F:Pn Rés. Vmc ms. 6), which contains bass lines to several of the pieces in the Florence mandola manuscript xix 29. I suggest that there might also be a connection between these and the Caccini manuscript.[3] The present location in Paris of both the Caccini manuscript (which is of Florentine provenance) and the continuo part-book (likely of Florentine provenance), coupled with the historical links between the courts of Tuscany and Paris, point to a strong Franco-Italian connection. Additional evidence of the French connection will be found further along in the Caccini manuscript.

In addition to, and following, the mandola section, there are two identical scale charts for an instrument tuned in fifths: e″, a′, d′, and g, exactly like a

---

[1] I:Fn Magl. xix 163, late 17th-cent., an incomplete ms. of his Kyrie and Gloria for four voices and instruments. Becherini (1959, 69).

[2] See G. Gaspari, *Catalogo della Biblioteca del Liceo Musicale di Bologna*, 3 (1893), 1097.

[3] Boetticher (1978, 268) notes a repertory connection between F:Pn Rés. Vmb ms. 4, Rés. Vmc ms. 5, and his Vmc ms. 6. In addition, I have noted that another continuo ms., I:Fn Magl. xix 110, also shares the same repertory. See Becherini 1959, 45–6.

violin (fos. 7ᵛ and 9ᵛ). As the mandoline, which also used this tuning (discussed fully in Part II), was not yet in existence, and since no other contemporary instrument except the violin is known to have used it at this time, these tuning charts are most likely for a violin. It is from this point in the manuscript (fo. 7) that the music becomes entirely single-line.

Although all the titles are written in Italian, some of the music in this section is French; for example, 'Amable' (fo. 16ᵛ) is the well-known 'Aimable Vainquer' by André Campra from his 'tragèdie lyrique', *Hesione* (1700). The piece is found in innumerable versions for many other instruments, as well as in the dance choreography books of the time. The 'Bure di Merline' is the 'Bourée d'Achille' from *Achille et Polixène* (1687) by Lully and Colasse. It became most popular as a dance from Louis Pecour's *Recueil de dances* (Paris, 1700).[4] The 'Gelosia' (fo. 23) is 'La Jalousie' found in Raoul Feuillet's *Recueil de contredanses* (Paris, 1706).

There is also an English connection in this section of the manuscript. 'Fullino' turns out to be one of the well-known pieces in John Playford's *The English Dancing Master* (London, 1651), entitled 'A la mode de France' or 'Nonesuch'.[5]

Other important concordances are found to the two dances on fos. 21ᵛ and 22ᵛ, 'Le Iogial' and 'La dani marca', which are also found in *Nuova e Curiosa Scuola de' Balli Theatrali* (Nuremburg, 1716) by the Venetian dancing master, Gregorio Lambranzi, as 'rogial' and 'animarca'. Lambranzi writes in the preface to his book that he has performed on the principal stages of France, Germany, and Italy, but nothing is known about him apart from his publication.[6] Though Lambranzi gives only the tunes to these pieces in his book, Caccini also provides the bass parts.

Amid the single-line music (fo. 11), Caccini also includes a scale chart for the psaltery or dulcimer ('scala per il salterio'). The inclusion of this chart in a manuscript which is, after all, a miscellany, may have absolutely nothing to do with the music in the manuscript, or it may be that some of the single-line music was intended to be played on the psaltery.

Up to this point in our exploration of music sources for the mandola/

---

[4] See the modern edition: Anne L. Witherell, *Louis Pecour's 1700 Recueil de dances* (Ann Arbor, 1983, 265).

[5] See Jeremy Barlow (ed.), *The Complete Country Dance Tunes from Playford's Dancing Master (1651–c.1728)* (London, 1985), nos. 2 and 71.

[6] *New Grove* (1980) 10: 401. A facs. ed. of the 1716 book is available (Leipzig, 1975).

mandolino, we have only encountered short, individual dance pieces or popular tunes, and not the more extended musical forms, the suites and sonatas, which made up a large portion of the lute, violin, and keyboard repertories from this period. The manuscript which was to mark a change in the nature of the instrument's repertory dates from the beginning of the eighteenth century, and represents the mandolino music of two Italian composers at the Habsburg court in Vienna; Francesco Conti (Contini) and Filippo Sauli. This manuscript (actually two manuscripts since there is a separate bass part of four folios which goes with the first item in the main manuscript) is found in the University Library in Prague (CS-ČSSR:Pu II KK 36). Until recently, it was thought to have been lost during the last world war, but, happily, it has now reappeared and is again available.[7] Its contents were described, somewhat inaccurately, by Johannes Wolf (1919, 123–4), so a new description of its contents is perhaps in order.

The main manuscript is in French tablature on four-line staves for a four-course instrument. Following the modern pagination, the contents are:

p. 1 'Sonata al Mandolino solo dal Signor Francesco Contini'. 'Arpeggio, Allemande, Sarabande, Minuet'.

p. 6 'Partita per C.C. di Sauli Filippo per il Mandolino'. 'Allemanda, Sarabanda, Courrante, Bourée, Gigue, Menuete'.

p. 14 'Partita di Filippo Sauli'. 'Prelude, Allemande, Sarabande, Courrente, Gigue, Gavotte, Menuete'.

p. 22 [Partita] 'Preludio per re sol fa ut., Allemande, Courrente, Aria Adagio, Giga, Menuet'.

p. 32 [Partita] 'Preludio, Allemande, Sarabande, Corrente, Giga'.

p. 38 'Partita per g sol re ut. di Filippo Sauli'. 'Ouverture, Allemande, Corrente, Sarabanda, Giga'.

p. 46 'Partita di Filippo Sauli'. 'Fuga, Allemanda, Corrente, Aria Adagio, Giga'.

The auxiliary manuscript contains just a sparsely-figured bass line entitled 'Basso per il Mandolino. Sonata dal Signore Francesco Contini'. This, of course, is the continuo accompaniment to the first item. There are no basses for any of the other pieces. The tuning used for the Contini sonata is shown by the tablature intervals and by the key of the bass to be g'', d'', a', e', the standard tuning for the mandolino. The remaining pieces depart from this in that the fourth course is tuned to only a major third below the third course.

[7] Boetticher (1978, 315) lists it as lost from its original location in Roudnice (Lobkowitz Library). I am indebted to Nigel North for his microfilm copy from Prague.

From the keys indicated by the solmization symbols in two of the items (pp. 22 and 30), this tuning must be g″, d″, a′, f′, and represents the only departure from the standard tuning in fourths that I have encountered in the Italian repertory.[8] The chord configurations in the tablatures show that all the pieces were played finger-style.

Francesco Conti (sometimes Contini, 1681–1732), was an important theorbist at the Habsburg court from 1701 and was officially designated court composer in 1713. It is not known whether he was related to the Agnolo Conti of the mid-seventeenth-century Florentine manuscripts. Franceso wrote some instrumental music and many cantatas, oratorios, and operas; on one of the latter, *Galatea vendicata* (1719) he employed the mandolino.* He was considered one of the most important composers of his day (*New Grove* 4: 680–1). Very little is known of Filippo Sauli, except that he was a colleague of Conti's at the Vienna court (Zuth 1926, 242), and that, like Conti and many other composers and players of the mandola/mandolino, he was also a theorbist. Their sonatas and partitas are well worth the attention of today's performers.

The Conti(ni) and Sauli manuscript was written at a time when the mandolino was being used increasingly in operas, oratorios, and other large-scale works. The personnel lists of various ensembles of the late seventeenth century, which included mandola players, have already been mentioned in Chapter 2, as has Alessandro Scarlatti's 1699 cantata with instruments including the mandola. In the eighteenth century, there developed what might almost be termed a convention: the aria with mandolino obbligato. Here are some notable examples of these arias, written by important composers, and included in their large-scale vocal works: Francesco Mancini's opera *Alessandro il Grande in Sidone* (1706) has an aria entitled 'Scherza l'alma . . .' for soprano with mandolino obbligato and continuo (I:Mc, V50. 10); Antonio Vivaldi's oratorio *Juditha triumphans* (1716) has a superb aria, 'Transit aetas', for mezzo-soprano, violins, an obbligato mandolino, and continuo (see Appendix II, Example 4); Johann Fux in *Diana Placata* (1717) includes the aria 'Si vedrà quel nome altero', which employs the 'citarina, o mandolino'; Antonio Lotti's *Teofane* (1719) contains an aria in the second

---

[8] There is one example in the mandore repertory as well: one section of the Scottish Skene Manuscript. See Tyler 1981a, 27–8.

* Professor Hermione Williams informs me that a mandolino is also called for in Conti's *Il Gioseffo* (1706), and that two mandolini are indicated in the score of his *Il Trionfo dell' Amicizia* (1711/1723).

act which is accompanied by a mandolino.[9] Francesco Conti's use of the mandolino in *Galatea vendicata* (1719) has already been mentioned. The aria 'Dolce sembiance il tuo rigore' in Francesco Gasparini's *Lucio vero* (1719) is for soprano, two violins, mandola, and continuo. The mandola part is for a high-pitched instrument with a range of g'–c''' in the treble clef (GB:Lbl Add. 24305, fos. 12ᵛ–15). Leonardo Vinci employed two mandolinos in the large orchestra for his serenata *La Contesa dei Numi* (1729) (D-ddr:Bds Landsberg 280a). Likewise, George Frideric Handel includes a charming mandolino obbligato part in the orchestral texture for the aria 'Hark! he strikes the golden lyre' from his English oratorio *Alexander Balus* (1748); Gioacchino Cocchi's aria 'Così e sior canapiolo' from an unknown opera of 1754, is for soprano, two violins, viola, mandolino, and continuo (GB:Lbl Add. 31654, fos. 117–118ᵛ). Johann Adolf Hasse, whose mandolino concerto will be discussed later in this chapter, has an aria 'Se un core ardi' with mandolino obbligato in his opera *Achille in Sciro* (1759) (I:Mc Q 8. 23). In Rinaldo di Capua's opera *La Donna Vendicativa* (1771), there is an aria, 'Sià la notte', which is scored for orchestra, four voices, 'calasione' (written in the bass clef for this long-necked member of the lute family, usually colascione), and mandola (GB:Lbl. Add. 16116, fos. 78ᵛ–96ᵛ). The mandola part, written in the treble clef, has a range of d'–d''' and a few closely-spaced chords typical of those for the mandolino.

This represents only the tip of the iceberg: the enormous body of surviving eighteenth-century opera scores has, as yet, hardly been explored. When it is, there will doubtless be many more examples found which demonstrate the mandolino's use in large-scale vocal repertory.

Gabinetto armonico (Rome, 1722), a kind of 'coffee-table' picture book of instruments with a few words of description, was the work of Filipo Bonani, a librarian rather than a music theorist or musician. In it, Bonani describes the mandola as a little instrument, commonly known by that name, but called mandora by the ancient Latins, having four single strings and producing a very high sound. He then discusses its etymology, deriving the word from pandora, which he says was the instrument of the ancient Assyrians.[10] His plate (no. 99) shows a small, flat-backed, guitar-shaped instrument

---

[9] See Douglas Alton Smith, 'Sylvius Leopold Weiss' in *Early Music*, 8 (1980), 50.

[10] Bonani's original reads: 'liii Mandola. Il piccolo Istrumento qui espresso, detto volgarmente Mandola, e dalli Latini Mandora, hà solamente quattro corde, e rende suono molto acuto. Un simil'istromento trovo essere stato usato dagl'Assiri, ma di tre corde, e chiamato Pandora. . . .' (p. 99.)

about the size of a modern ukelele with four strings (Tyler 1980, 110). He also describes another instrument, which he calls the pandura, telling us that this is the name the Neapolitans used for an instrument like the mandola, but differing from the latter in that it is much larger, is strung with eight strings of metal, is played with a plectrum, and renders a full sound.[11] He provides an illustration of his 'pandura' (plate 97), which shows a lute-like, round-backed instrument, with a fairly large body, a flat soundboard, and a very long neck; it has a sickle-shaped peg-box and ten pegs for ten strings (rather than the eight in his verbal description). The vagaries and inaccuracies in all of Bonani's engravings make it difficult to come to any conclusions about the instruments he describes, and certainly, his equating of the mandola with a little guitar is not supported by other sources. However, even taking his unreliability into account, it could possibly be that the large instrument—which, he says, the Neapolitans called a 'pandura'—with its metal strings played with a plectrum, was a forerunner of the Neapolitan mandoline (though the small mandoline size is not encountered until after *c*.1750; see Part II).

In the Rome of Bonani's time, the mandola was a popular enough instrument for the music publisher Antonio Cleton to publish two collections of solo sonatas, for which the mandola is named as one of the treble instruments which can be used to perform them. (Both books are published in facsimile by Studio per Edizione Scelte, Florence.) The first is Giuseppe Gaetano Boni's *Divertimenti per camera a violino, violone, cembalo, flauto, e mandola*, Op. 2 (Rome, *c*.1725), and the second, Roberto Valentini's *Sonate per il flauto traversiero, col basso che possano servise per violino, mandola et oboe*, Op. 12 (Rome, 1730). There are twelve solo sonatas from Boni and six from Valentini, all of which are printed in score in the format of treble clef solo line and figured bass line for the continuo accompaniment. Boni's title-page implies that the violin, bass viol (or cello), and harpsichord combination is the first choice for performance, but that the recorder (flauto) or the mandola could be used instead of the violin. Valentini's title-page implies that the transverse flute and continuo are the first choice, but that either the violin, mandola, or oboe could be used in place of the flute. The music in both collections is written idiomatically for the violin and the flute respect-

---

[11] Bonani's original reads: 'xlix Pandura. Pandura si dice dalli Napolitani l'istromento seguente, la forma di cui è poco differente dalla Mandola, mà è di mole molto più grande; è armato di otto corde di metallo, e si suona con la penna, e rende grata armonia.' (p. 97.)

ively, but can be played effectively on a six-course mandola/mandolino with minimal adaptation (of such details as the manner of playing the slurs marked in the music).

Boni was a highly successful Bolognese musician, who came to Rome sometime between 1711 (the date of Corelli's favourable reply to a letter from an intermediary, asking him to introduce Boni into Roman musical circles) and 1717 (the date of Boni's first Roman publication) (Castellani 1985, Introduction). Very Corellian in style, the sonatas in Boni's *Divertimenti* are first-class examples of the baroque solo sonata, and deserve to be performed before concert audiences today.

Valentini was actually an English flautist, Robert Valentine (*c*.1680–*c*.1735), who lived and worked in Rome. A considerable number of his compositions, mostly solo and trio sonatas, were published during his lifetime, and his music was widely known throughout Europe. Though Valentine was not nearly as fine a composer as Boni, his 1730 sonatas are worth exploring.

The mandolino also seems to have found a small amount of favour in London, where two similar collections of music were published. The first is Willem Defesch's *XX Canzonette a voce sola di soprano col basso continuo, da potersi suonare con violino, flauto traversa, e mandolino* (London, *c*.1745), a collection of Italian songs in the treble clef with figured bass. The title-page implies that these songs could be performed instrumentally by replacing the singer with a violin, flute, or mandolino. The other publication is Nicolas Cloes's *One Hundred French Songs set for a Voice, German Flute, Violin, Harpsichord and Pandola* (London, 1749). Despite its misleading title-page, the music again consists of just a treble clef vocal line and a figured bass for the harpsichord. The other instruments are alternatives to the voice. The term 'pandola' is found in no other source and presumably refers to the mandola.

Antonio Vivaldi (1678–1741) is one of the best-known baroque composers to today's concert-going and record-buying public, and his delightful concerto for two mandolins and strings (RV532)[12] has become a frequently heard item in concert programmes, in television commercials, on film soundtracks, and, of course, on record. Vivaldi wrote for an incredibly wide variety of instruments, including the Italian lute[13] and the mandolino. He

[12] See Ryom (1986) under the various RV numbers for accurate descriptions of each work.

[13] See Ch. 2, n. 14. The lute in 18th-cent. Italy retained its traditional Renaissance tuning (g′, d′,

taught music and directed performances at the Venetian Ospedale della Pietà, which was originally an orphanage, but which had become, by Vivaldi's time, a convent school for girls, with a long tradition of developing the musical talents of the girls and widely renowned for its musical performances.

The girls of the Pietà were able to play a wide range of instruments, including the chalumau ('salmoè'), the viol ('viola all'inglese'), theorbo, lute, and mandolino, as well as violins, violas, etc. This fact doubtless inspired Vivaldi to write some of the remarkably colourful music for which he is known. In his oratorio *Juditha triumphans*, RV645 (1716) for example, the girls played two recorders, two oboes, soprano chalumau, two clarinets, two trumpets with timpani, four theorbos, organ, five viols, viola d'amore, strings, continuo, and mandolino.

It is not known when precisely he wrote the solo concerto, 'Con[cer]to p[er] Mandolino' RV425, or the double concerto, 'Con[cer]to p[er] 2 Mandolini' RV532, but they were undoubtedly written for his musical forces at the Pietà, probably in the 1730s. The solo concerto is for mandolino, two violins, viola, and a basso continuo line (for cello?) and an unspecified chordal continuo instrument. The mandolino part is entirely single-line with no chords, and the range is c'–c''', which would be playable on a five-course instrument tuned in fourths throughout: g'', d'', a', e', b. As there is as yet no Italian evidence for playing the mandolino with a plectrum, Vivaldi's works are presumably intended for finger-style technique and, indeed, the mandolino parts can be played very comfortably with the fingers. For the left hand, the parts allow for considerable use of open strings and much of the writing

a, f, c, G) for the first six courses, plus a varying number of further bass courses from two extra (on an eight-course lute with a single peg-box) to seven extra (on a thirteen-course lute with a second extended neck to carry the basses). The larger instrument was known as the 'arcileuto' or just as frequently by the simple name 'leuto'. For example, Giovanni Zamboni's collection of sonatas in tablature (Lucca, 1718) is for a thirteen-course instrument which he calls 'Leuto'. Many modern performers have been confused as to the lute intended by Vivaldi for his music and, because the music is mostly written in the treble clef, have assumed it is to be played in the same register as the violin. They have ignored the fact that Vivaldi has the lute play from the bass clef as a continuo instrument (see RV540 and RV556) when it is not playing its solo passages from the treble clef. This confusion has led some eminent performers to play Vivaldi's lute pieces on a mandolino which, for their purposes, they call a soprano lute. One such performer in his recording of music by Vivaldi for lute and mandolin, only differentiates between the lute music and the mandolin music by playing the former finger-style and the latter with a plectrum. As it should be fairly clear to readers of this book, the mandolino of Vivaldi's time was also normally played finger-style.

is in the comfortable first position, if the proper tuning in fourths, mentioned above, is used.

The double concerto is for two mandolinos, two violins, viola, and a basso continuo line assumed to be for cello, which plays along with the specified organ. Again, the mandolino parts have no chords, but the ranges extend down to g below the treble clef (g–d‴), which suggests that six-course instruments are required, tuned as follows: g″, d″, a′, e′, b, g. With this tuning, there are, again, many opportunities for the use of open strings, such as in the passage in pedal point in the first movement (bars 56–60) where the open low e′ courses can be used quite effectively. Indeed, when the proper mandolino tuning is used and the music played finger-style, it becomes clear that Vivaldi was making a special point of exploiting as many of the idiomatic resources of the mandolino as possible in this music, and the remarkably clear, ringing tone of the mandolino comes to the fore in a way never heard in performances using other types of mandolin.

These concertos seem to be 'chamber' concertos, that is, they were intended to be performed by just the number of instruments called for in the manuscripts, one to a part, rather than by a larger force of orchestral strings. Considering the relatively soft volume of the mandolino, a non-orchestral accompaniment would make sense. Certainly, there is no evidence that the term 'concerto' in Vivaldi's time meant orchestral doubling as a matter of course, unless the term 'concerto grosso' is used. Rather, the Italian 'concerto' can simply translate into English as consort, a small ensemble of as few as two players.[14] This consideration, along with the rediscovery of the character, playing techniques, and timbres of instruments such as the mandolino, forms an important basis for the interpretation and realistic performance of baroque music today.

Vivaldi used two mandolinos in a wonderfully colourful concerto (RV558) for 'due flauti, due tiorbe, due mandolini, due salmò, due violini in tromba marina, et un violoncello' (two recorders, two theorbos, two mandolinos, two chalumaux, two violins modified in some way to imitate the tromba marina, and a cello) as the solo instruments, in addition to the accompanying four-part strings and continuo. Each pair of instruments alternates with the other pairs in bursts of solo playing between the tutti ritornellos. The

---

[14] See, for example, the 'concertos' for solo mandolino and continuo accompaniment by Fontanelli and Vaccari in I:Bc ms. EE 155.

memorable tune in the slow middle movement is played by just the solo violins in unison with the two mandolinos. The two fast movements are very jolly and dance-like. While perhaps not one of Vivaldi's greatest works, this concerto is certainly an apt accompaniment to a festive occasion, and, in fact, we know the exact occasion on which it was played. It was a performance to honour the visit to the Pietà of Frederick Christian, the Prince-Elector of Saxony, on 21 March 1740. The concerto was one of four instrumental works (and one vocal work) played before the Elector. (One of the other works was Vivaldi's beautiful concerto for viola d'amore and lute, RV540.)

In a letter of 26 December 1736 to Marchese Guido Bentivoglio, one of Vivaldi's patrons in Ferrara, the composer, with the obvious intent of obtaining a commission, asks if Bentivoglio still enjoys playing the mandolino. In Bentivoglio's reply, dated four days later, the Marchese confesses that he takes out his mandolino only once a year, or even less (Talbot 1984, 85–6). Bentivoglio's reply is perhaps part of the reason why there isn't more mandolino music by Vivaldi, and one can only feel the utmost regret that it wasn't lost in the post!

It was in 1740 that the Elector of Saxony, Frederick Christian, visited Venice and heard Vivaldi's music at the Pietà. Following his visit, he was able to take back with him to his Dresden court a souvenir score of the instrumental music he heard performed (D-ddr:Dlb 2389/o/4 no. 1).[15] At his court, the Elector employed one of the greatest baroque composers of the eighteenth century, Johann Adolf Hasse (1699–1783). Hasse was admired throughout Europe for his Italian vocal music, in particular his enormous output of operas (though, by most standards, his instrumental output is considerable as well) (*New Grove* 8: 279–93). Nicknamed 'il Sassone' (the Saxon), Hasse had at his disposal the renowned Dresden court orchestra; he also had complete control over the city's opera productions.

Among his instrumental works is a 'Concerto con Mandolino obligato. del Sig.r Sassone', in the library in East Berlin where much of the Dresden court music is now to be found. The concerto (D-ddr:Bds Landsberg 313/8) is for two violins, mandolino, and continuo. It is in the Vivaldian form of three movements (Allegro, Largo, Allegro) and appears to be another small-scale chamber concerto of great charm. Like Vivaldi's, Hasse's mandolino

---

[15] A fascimile edition of the entire MS was published by the Zentralantiquariat Der Deutschen Demokratischen Republik, (Leipzig, 1978).

part is entirely single-line. The date of the concerto is not known, but it must be before 1741, the date when movements one and three (with a different second movement) were published as no. 11 in the London edition entitled *Twelve Concertos in Six Parts, for the German Flute, Two Violins, a Tenor, with a Thorough Bass for the Harpsichord or Violoncelle*, Op. 3 (London, 1741). As we see, the flute version of the concerto, as published in London, has an added viola ('tenor') part. The violin parts, the flute (mandolino) part, and the continuo bass line, are the same as in the mandolino version (with the exception, as has been noted, of the slow middle movement). The same concerto was mistakenly attributed to Pergolesi in the 1762–87 Breitkopf catalogues.[16]

An anonymous Viennese manuscript from the mid-eighteenth century should be mentioned (A:Wn Ms. Mus. 1082). It contains preludes, contre-dances, minuets, and other dance forms in staff notation. No composers are named. On fo. 1, in what appears to be a later hand, are the words 'pour les cistre' [sic]. Yet fo. 1^v has, in staff notation, the tuning g″, d″, a′, e′, b, f, which corresponds to no known cistre (or 'English guittar') tuning, but which is, of course (apart from the lowered sixth course), the standard mandolino tuning. It seems likely, therefore, that 'cistre' is a mis-labelling and that this is possibly another collection for the mandolino.

Whether or not this Vienna manuscript is for mandolino, from the mid-eighteenth century onwards, mandolino music generally consisted of the more extensive forms: the sonata, quartet, and concerto. This repertory is found in increasing amounts in such libraries as the Biblioteca Comunale in Assisi, which has a 'Sonata a Mandolino e Basso di F. Giuseppe Paolucci' (I: Ac N.17/2) and twelve 'Sonate a due Mandolini e Basso' by the same composer (I:Ac N.178/1) (Sartori 1962, 312). Paolucci (1726–76) was a composer and theorist who, at one point in his career (1756–69), was Maestro di Capella at Santa Maria Gloriosa dei Frari in Venice (*New Grove* 14: 166). His mandolino works are apparently from this Venetian period, since the sonatas for two mandolinos are dated 1758, 1759, and 1761 and the solo sonata is dated 1769.

There is another large collection in the Conservatory Library in Milan (I: Mc). The manuscripts include 'Sonata per Mandolino del Sigr.e Gaetano

---

[16] Drummond (1980, 251). *New Grove* (1980) 8: 292 states that the concerto is in Munich (D-brd: Mbs), but this is apparently an error. A modern edition by K. Wölki was published in Cologne in 1958.

Monza', 'Sinfonia per la Mandòla, del Sig.r Fran[cesc]o Piccone', 'Pastorale' (anonymous, Piccone?), and 'Sonata del Sig.r Bonaventura Terreni'. These are for solo mandola/mandolino with a bass for continuo. There is also a 'Minuetto del Sig.r Bonaventura Terreni' for 'amandolino' with a written-out accompaniment for 'cembalo'. In addition, there is a 'Studio per la Mandola di Francesco Piccone' which is actually for two instruments, both parts written in treble clef, and a 'Sinfonia a due Mandole e Basso' by Nicola Romaldi (1680–1740). I can find no information on any of these composers, except for Romaldi, who probably worked in Rome, where he collaborated with Carlo Cesarini and Giuseppe Valentini in composing the music for the opera *La Finta Rapita* (1714) (*New Grove* 19: 496). The pieces, all in the treble clef for the solo instrument(s), have a number of chords which are in the closely-spaced configurations for mandolino tuning, and which also indicate a finger-style technique.

A recently acquired collection of manuscripts is in Florence in the library of Maestro Marco Fornaciari (ex Zannerini Collection, Trieste). It is a large collection of mid-eighteenth-century Italian instrumental music which includes several lute manuscripts, a 'salterio' manuscript, and five manuscripts for mandolino.[17] Of great interest is the first of the five, a 'Sonata per Armandolino del Sig.r Gio. Batt.a S. Martino'. This spelling of the composer's name is one commonly found for Giovanni Battista Sammartini (*c*.1701–75), and, judging by the musical style and quality of the sonata, it seems most likely that this gem of a piece for our instrument is, indeed, by one of the major figures of baroque music.[18]

The sonata, in G major, has three movements (Allegro 2/4, Andante 2/4, [Allegro] 3/4). It is replete with passages in thirds, arpeggios, and pedal points, and has several chords which would be virtually impossible to play on an instrument with any but mandolino tuning. The range, going down to g below the treble clef, requires a six-course instrument, and the layout of some of the chords indicates finger-style technique. The score is in the format of treble clef, with unfigured bass clef for the continuo accompaniment. The term 'armandolino' (like the term 'amandolino') is occasionally encoun-

---

[17] Virtually all this important collection is unknown to musicological literature. I am indebted to Maestro Fornaciari for allowing me a brief examination of the collection.

[18] For information on Sammartini, see *New Grove* (1980) 16: 452–7. An incomplete piece for lute is found in I:Bc EE 155 (facs. edn. p. 84). It is entitled 'Suonata di Monseur Martino Milanese per Arcileuto Francese'. This is likely to be by Sammartini as well.

tered in other sources, and, in this case, seems to signify nothing more than a regional spelling variant, there being nothing in the music to suggest that it is any different from other music for the mandolino. Sammartini's sonata is a major addition to the mandolino repertory (see Appendix II, Example 5).

The remaining four manuscripts in the Fornaciari collection are all anonymous. The titles are 'Sonata di Armandolino è Basso', 'Sonata a Mandolino a primo, e Basso', 'Sonata a Primo e Basso', and 'Sonata'. All have similar musical characteristics and features, and the first may be another by Sammartini.

In Venice (Biblioteca Nazionale Marciana) there are six 'suonatine' for mandolino and continuo, and one for two mandolinos and continuo, by Girolamo Venier. A scale chart in this manuscript confirms it is for a mandolino tuned g″, d″, a′, e′, b.

The city of Bologna was one of the great musical centres of the seventeenth and eighteenth centuries. With its many churches, such as San Petronio, employing a glittering array of composers and musicians, its important opera theatres, municipal orchestra, music publishers, and music academies, including the famous Accademia Filarmonica, Bologna could well be considered the equal in music activity to Rome and Venice.

For our study, a highly interesting Bolognese document survives. Entitled 'Suonate di Celebri Auttori . . .' ('Sonatas of Celebrated Composers'), it is a collection of lute and some mandolino music, compiled by a Bolognese archlute and theorbo player (and painter) called Filippo Dalla Casa (I:Bc EE 155).[19] The dates 1759 and 1760 appear in the manuscript, though some of the music must be much older since certain of the composers represented, such as Tinazzoli, died as early as 1730. The mandolino pieces are:

'Suonata à Mandolino, è Arcileuto obligati del Sig.r Antonio Tinazzoli.' (a one-movement sonata)
'Concerto à Mandolino, è Basso del Arcileuto di Giuseppe Vaccari' (Allegro, Andante, Allegro)
'Concerto à Mandolino, è Basso del Arcileuto di Giuseppe Vaccari' (Allegro, Andante, Giga)
'Concerto à Mandolino, è Basso del Arcileuto di Ludovico Fontanelli' (Allegro, Andante, Allegro)
'Suonata con Grave, è suo Minuetto à Mandola è Basso del Arcileuto' [anon.] (Allegro, Adagio, Minuetto)

[19] The entire manuscript is published in facsimile by Studio Per Edizioni Scelte (Florence, 1984) with an introduction by Orlando Cristoforetti.

All the pieces are in the format of a score in treble clef for the mandolino, and bass clef for the continuo accompaniment by the archlute. Although the name of the instrument changes in the title of the last item, the music is identical in range and style to the others, and it is therefore probably just another example of the ambiguity of terms which has characterized the story of our instrument so far. All the pieces have arpeggios, rapid scale passages, ostinato passages which favour open courses, and chord configurations suitable for mandolino tuning and finger-style technique. The tuning is confirmed in the second portion of the manuscript (entitled 'Regole di Musica . . .') where, along with scale charts for the 'Tiorba' and 'Arcileuto Francese', is one for the 'Mandolino', which shows it to be tuned g″, d″, a′, e′, b. This five-course instrument suffices for the Vaccari and Fontanelli pieces, but the Tinazzoli and anonymous pieces call for a low g and hence a sixth course.

I have been unable to find any information about Giuseppe Vaccari, but Antonio Tinazzoli's name is found in the records of the Accademia Filarmonica, where it is noted that he was elected to that organization in 1673, was a Bolognese singer and music teacher, and died in 1730.[20] These same records shows that there were many other lute, theorbo, and mandolino players elected to the Accademia: for example, Francesco Conti (previously discussed) elected in 1708, and Carlo Arrigoni (1697–1744) elected in 1722 (*New Grove* 1: 636–7), who has left a concerto for mandolino (US:Wc).

Lodovico Fontanelli (*c.*1682–1748), elected to the Accademia in 1717, is another. Fontanelli was born in Bologna, but, as a young boy, began his musical studies in Florence with a teacher named Forni, who was a professor of theorbo and archlute. Fontanelli soon became an outstanding player, particularly of the theorbo, and on returning to Bologna, began a long and active career as a player and renowned teacher (Cristoforetti 1984, pp. v–vi). He was a member of the municipal orchestra from 1718 to the year of his death, 1748 (Gambassi 1984, 636). In addition to his concerto for mandolino and some lute music found elsewhere in the Dalla Casa manuscript, there are two manuscripts of music by him for the chittarone francese (a kind of theorboed guitar) now in the library of Robert Spencer.[21]

It is assumed that the Giovanni Giuseppe Fontanelli listed as a player of the lute, theorbo, and mandolino in the Bologna municipal orchestra from

---

[20] Cristoforetti (1984, p. v). One of his many students was his nephew, the better-known Agostino Tinazzoli.

[21] Robert Spencer, 'The Chitarrone Francese' in *Early Music*, 4 (1976) 164–6.

1726–77 (Gambassi 1984, 636), is Lodovico's son. As well as a player, Gio-vanni was also a fine instrument maker, as is attested to by his surviving three mandolinos and a lute. One of the mandolinos (not a 'mandore' as labelled by the museum), is dated 1726 and is in the Van Raalte Collection (no. 39) in Kilmarnock, Scotland.[22] Another, a six-course mandolino (not a 'pandurina' as labelled by the museum) dated 1762, is in Washington, Smithsonian Institute (no. 60. 1353) (Pohlmann 1975, 371; Lütgendorff 1922), while the third, found in Paris in the collection of the Conservatoire National de Musique (F:Pc no. E41. C.244), is a six-course mandolino (not a 'luth soprano' as labelled by the museum) dated 1771. (The lute is in the Musée Instrumentale, Nice, where it is correctly labelled!)

There are several other mandolinists worth mentioning who are listed as members of the municipal orchestra from this period to the end of the century: Cristoforo Babbi (Balbi) is listed as playing the mandolino (sometimes listed as 'mandola') from 1774–84; Stanislao Chiusoli from 1782–7; Onofrio Mandini, in 1786; Giuseppe Marchignoli from 1773–97; Nicola Gaetano Minghelli from 1785–7; and Melchiorre Prosperi, in 1796 (Gambassi 1984, 633, 635, 637–9).

From the evidence examined so far, it is clear that finger-style playing was the norm for the mandolino in Italy, and I can find no evidence for plectrum-style playing until the second half of the eighteenth century. It is reasonable to assume, however, that, even earlier, in the context of an opera performed in a theatre with the mandolino as part of the orchestra, some mandolino players might prefer to use a plectrum in order to produce a louder sound. By the second half of the century, the new Neapolitan-style mandoline was gaining popularity (albeit first in France), and the competi-tion from the louder, plectrum-played instrument undoubtedly influenced traditional mandolino players to adopt the plectrum as well.

The first firm evidence of plectrum-playing on the mandolino is found in the tutor published in Paris in 1771 by Giovanni Fouchetti: *Méthode pour apprendre facilement a jouer de la Mandoline à 4 et à 6 Cordes*.[23] All the music in the tutor is for the four-course Neapolitan mandoline; however, Fouchetti discusses the six-course mandolino in his preliminary instructions (pp. 5–8), and, somewhat surprisingly, states that he prefers it. According to Fou-

---

[22] John Downing, 'An Inventory of the Charles van Raalte Collection of Instruments', *Fellowship of Makers and Restorers of Historical Instruments* (*FOMRHI*) *Quarterly*, 24, (July 1981), 58, 65.

[23] Facsimile published by Minkoff Reprint (Geneva, 1983).

chetti, the six-course instrument has six pairs of strings tuned g″, d″, a′, e′, b, g. The strings are of gut or metal, according to personal preference. His instructions for plectrum technique apply to either instrument. (See Chapter 9 for an explanation of Fouchetti's plectrum technique.) The fact that both Fouchetti's tutor and Michel Corrette's *Nouvelle Méthode* (Paris, 1772) include the mandolino as an alternative to the Neapolitan mandoline, indicates that, by this time, in addition to its own earlier, finger-style repertory, the six-course mandolino, played with a plectrum and with a few minor adjustments to the chord configurations in the music, also had the entire repertory of the Neapolitan mandoline to play! (See Appendix III.)

Though a few of the late mandolino sources still imply finger-style playing, the sources from the last part of the eighteenth century are probably intended for the plectrum-style which Fouchetti's tutor advocates. One such source is Giovanni Hoffman's printed collection of *Tre duetti per il Mandolino, e Violino*, Op. 1 (Vienna, 1799). The mandolino part is in the treble clef as, of course, is the violin part. The duets, three fine sonatas, are, in fact, excellent examples of Viennese chamber music from the age of Beethoven. The mandolino part has five- and six-note closely-spaced chords which leave no doubt that it is for a standard, six-course instrument. The chords here, however, unlike those in earlier sources, are all arranged so that they can be played on consecutive courses. This implies plectrum-style playing.

I can find no information about Giovanni Hoffmann's life or career, which is a pity since he has left several other fine compositions for mandolino. These are found in the library of the Gesellschaft der Musikfreunde in Vienna, and include a concerto for mandolino, two violins, viola, two oboes, two horns, and 'basso'; two quartets for mandolino, violin, viola, and cello; a 'Cassazione' for two mandolinos and cello; four divertimentos for mandolino, violin, and 'basso'; three sonatas for mandolino and 'basso'; two sonatas for two mandolinos; and a serenade for mandolino and viola.

This wonderfully rich Viennese collection also contains chamber music for mandolino by Melchior Chiesa, Georg Druschetzky, Dolphin, Giuseppe Blesber, and Johann Conrad Schlik, including solo and duo sonatas with one or two mandolinos and continuo; mandolino duets; and trios with mandolino, violin, and cello. (See Appendix I for further details.)

One final composer represented in the same collection is Giovanni Francesco Giuliani (*c*.1760–*c*.1818), who spent most of his professional life in Florence where he wrote music for the stage as well as a great deal of instrumental music, including concertos for cello, for violin, and for harpsichord; sonatas for various instruments; and quartets. Among the quartets in the Vienna collection are his 'VI Quartetti per Mandolino, Violino e Violoncello ò Viola e Liuto'. Unlike most of the mandolin music in this collection, the Giuliani quartets, to judge by their chord configurations, appear to be for the Neapolitan mandoline, and it may be, therefore, that all the Giuliani sources discussed here are for that instrument.

In the six Vienna quartets, the mandolin and violin play in equal ranges from the treble clef, and the viola plays the third part from the alto clef. The fourth part, for the lute, is written in the bass clef, except for its solo passages, which are written in the treble clef but sound an octave lower. The lute used at this time had a lute-shaped body, a guitar-like neck, and a sickle-shaped peg-box for six pairs of strings tuned to guitar intervals and pitches (see the section in Chapter 5 on the large mandola and mandora). As there is

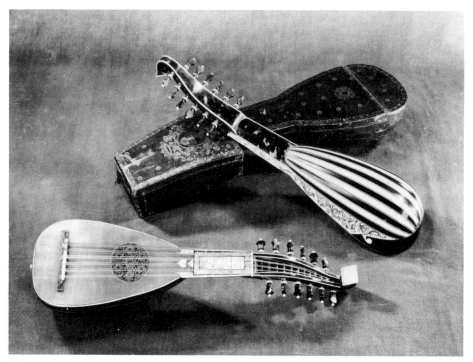

Illustration 4. Two mandolinos, Giovanni Smorsone, 1736, and Domenico Brambilla, 1768.

no separate part for the cello, it must have been, as Giuliani's title suggests, an alternate choice for the viola parts.

There is another set of six quartets by Giuliani for two mandolins, viola, and lute in the Seminario Library in Lucca, together with a set of six more quartets for two mandolins, flute, and cello and a further set of six quartets for two mandolins, flute, and viola. Curiously, the third and fifth quartets of this last set are ascribed elsewhere to Alessandro Rolla in a set of two quartets (here called sonatas) for 'Flauto, due Amandolini, una Viola' (I:Gi(l) SS.B.1.1 (H.8)). This ascription to Rolla seems highly unlikely under the circumstances.

One final source of Giuliani's music is in the library of Robert Spencer. It is a manuscript bass or lute part-book ('Basso o Liuto') for a set of six duo sonatas, 'Sei Sonate a due Mandolini e Basso'. The two mandolin parts are, unfortunately, lost.

The extensive mandolino repertory in the Vienna collection, including the chamber works for mandolino by Giovanni Hoffmann, all from the very end of the eighteenth century, marks a high point in the serious use of the mandolino before its general decline in the following century.

Today, though the instrument survives in the twentieth century as the 'mandolino milanese' or 'mandolino lombardo',[24] it is not generally known to concert audiences. This is a great pity since, in an era of music performance which is characterized by a resurgence of interest in baroque and early classical repertories, the mandolino, with its totally baroque tone-colour and its considerable repertory, has a significant contribution to make. It is my hope that this book will help to restore to music lovers today this delightful baroque resource.

---

[24] The mandolino has an unbroken history of use from the 17th-cent. to the present day, and, although the Neapolitan instrument now dominates, there are definite signs of renewed interest in the mandolino amongst players today. For an early 20th-cent. tutor for mandolino, see A. Pisani, *Manuale teorico pratico del mandolinista* (Milan, 1913). This also includes a bibliography of many other tutors from the 19th-cent.

4

Practical Information about the Mandolino for Players and Makers

Tuning and Stringing

The standard tuning of the mandolino from the seventeenth to the twentieth centuries is as follows:

Needless to say, for sources of four-course music, only the highest four notes are required; for five-course sources, only the highest five notes. The only exception to this tuning in the mandolino repertory occurs in the Contini and Sauli manuscript (CS-ČSSR:Pu II KK 36) in which items 2–7 require the fourth course to be tuned a semi-tone higher to f′.

From its earliest history, gut strings have been used on the mandolino, as they are still used on the Milanese mandolino today (though the modern instrument normally has six single strings). These were plain strings of different thicknesses, and, even when overspun or wound strings came into use in the second half of the seventeenth century, they were generally used only for the sixth and possibly for the fifth course(s). Modern nylon strings are a reasonable substitute for gut, and nylon does have the advantages of being readily available and lower in price. The use of gut, however, is becoming increasingly widespread amongst players of early instruments, such as the lute, and an excellent introduction to gut-stringing is the article 'Gut Strings' by Djilda Abbot and Ephraim Segerman, in *Early Music*, 4 (1976).

It is essential that the strings be fairly thin, and a suggested set of gauges for gut would be: (1) 0.38 mm; (2) 0.46 mm; (3) 0.60 mm; (4) 0.70 mm; (5) 0.80 mm; (6) a light flexible, wound string of about 0.72 mm in diameter (such as a Pyramid no. 1018). For general purposes, the fourth course could also be a Pyramid no. 905 (0.45 mm) and the fifth course a Pyramid no. 1010

(0.54 mm). These gauges are suitable for the typical mandolino string lengths of 29–32 cm. Gut strings, though less durable, produce strikingly brighter and more sonorous tones than nylon. This stringing can be used at today's standard of pitch (A440 HZ) or at the lower standards, such as A415 HZ, commonly used by specialists in baroque music.

In the latter part of the eighteenth century, metal strings are mentioned for the mandolino. Fouchetti (1771, 7) says gut or metal strings are used at this time, depending upon preference, but he gives no further details. Corrette (*Nouvelle méthode*, 1772, 3) also mentions the mandolino, and his tuning chart shows that the first four courses are doubled in unison, but that the fifth and sixth are doubled in octaves, one string of each pair being an octave higher than the fundamental note. He says the first and second are guitar 'chanterelles' (that is, gut strings), and the rest are 'clavecin' strings (metal). The third is a 'jaune' (brass) 'no. 5', the fourth is a 'demie fillés' (open-wound), and the fifth and sixth are 'filées en entier' (fully-wound). The fully-wound strings must, of course, be for the fundamental notes, but Corrette doesn't say what the upper octaves are. See Chapter 9 for more information on the stringings of Fouchetti and Corrette. It should be remembered that these two tutors are for plectrum-played instruments, and the metal stringing may be related to this technique.

Tablature

The majority of mandolin music is written in staff notation, but there are a handful of sources in Italian and French tablature, as indicated in the list of sources for the mandola/mandolino (see Appendix I). Tablature is a very simple and quickly-learned graphic notation for fretted instruments and, to facilitate an understanding of these sources, a conveniently available explanation can be found in Tyler, *The Early Guitar* (London, 1980, 63–6) or in the article 'Tablature', in the *New Grove Dictionary of Musical Instruments* (London, 1984).

Technique

Unlike the Neapolitan mandoline, the mandolino has no tutors from the period with which this book is concerned to guide us. Nineteenth- and twentieth-century tutors for mandolino all use plectrum technique, but in the seventeenth and eighteenth centuries we know that the mandolino was mainly played finger-style. The only eighteenth-century sources for plectrum-playing on the mandolino are Fouchetti (1771) and Corrette (1772), which have been previously mentioned. The plectrum technique found in these two sources is fully described in Chapter 9.

Finger-style technique for the right hand must have been similar to contemporary lute, theorbo, and guitar technique, and you will probably have noticed how frequently various mandolino composers are also cited as being lute or theorbo players. Of course, the widely-spread right-hand fingers, with the thumb ready to play ever more distant bass courses on the theorbo, must, for the mandolino, be considerably more contracted in order to manage the narrow spread of courses on the tiny mandolino. Also, the right-hand wrist must be more highly arched than on larger instruments so that the smallest area of the fingertips will be able to pluck the strings efficiently. The index and middle fingers, along with the thumb, but not the third finger, seem to be effective in the music, and in this respect, the right-hand technique would be similar to that described in many eighteenth-century guitar tutors (see Tyler 1980, 134–7).

Most contemporary lute, theorbo, and guitar players used the flesh of their fingertips for plucking the strings, but several used fingernails. We will probably never know if nails were used on the mandolino.

In the revival of the early mandolino, all right-hand technique will have to be a matter of experimentation, but, happily, there are today many fine lute players throughout the world from whom we can learn many things about early plucked instrument techniques.

For the left hand, the few sources which give fingerings show that the first, second, and third fingers are employed mainly, leaving the fourth finger for extensions and certain chords:

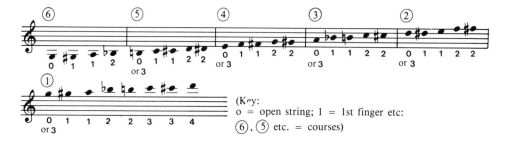

(Key:
o = open string; 1 = 1st finger etc:
⑥, ⑤ etc. = courses)

Ornaments

Seventeenth- and early eighteenth-century ornamentation is, I think, too vast a topic to be discussed here, except to mention that in all the mandolino repertory, only a very few ornament symbols are encountered in the music. Most of the ornamentation was left to the performer to add, be it sparsely or profusely. The symbols encountered are t., tr., or ·/. and the curved lines connecting groups of notes. The first three signs indicate, in Italian, a *trillo* or *tremolo*. These are ornaments applied to a single note and can be defined as short, melodic formulas gracing a particular note. The word *tremolo* in baroque writing does not refer to a specific ornament, but is a generic term meaning that some kind of an ornament should be played at that point. Which specific ornament, an upper-note or lower-note trill, a mordent, and so on, is left to the player to decide. Only in the latter part of the eighteenth century do the symbols come to mean more specific kinds of ornaments. (For these later ornaments, see Chapter 9.) The curved lines connecting groups of notes are slurs, which means that only the first note of the group is plucked with the right hand and the remaining ones are played with the left hand by 'pulling off' or 'hammering on', a common technique for guitar players.

It is interesting to note that along with the trill, mordent, and appoggiatura, the slur, vibrato, and arpeggio were considered as separate ornaments throughout much of the baroque era. A discussion of all these, especially as relating to Italian music for plucked instruments is found in Tyler, *The Early Guitar* (London, 1980, 87–102).

Much of the current and quite voluminous writings on baroque ornamentation are heavily biased towards French style, and few have concentrated on Italian ornamentation which is, of course, essential to the mandolino. One of the few works to give both sides of the stylistic picture and to differentiate between the two musical styles is Frederick Neumann's *Ornamentation in Baroque and Post-Baroque Music* (Princeton, 1978). See also the article 'Ornaments' by Donnington in the *New Grove Dictonary of Music and Musicians* (London, 1980).

Recordings

There are only a very few recordings available at present on which a proper mandolino can be heard. The only recording on which the mandolino is played using the appropriate finger-style technique is an Archiv recording (415 674–1) entitled *Alla Rustica*, which includes Vivaldi's concerto for two mandolins in G major, and his concerto in C major 'con molti stromenti'. There are two recordings on which proper mandolinos can be heard, but played with a plectrum; one is the Hyperion release (A66160) which includes the Vivaldi concertos for one and two mandolins, and the other is a Philips release (5614379) which contains another performance of the Vivaldi concerto for two mandolins.

Surviving Instruments

There is a surprisingly large number of original mandolinos from the seventeenth and eighteenth centuries to be found in museums and collections around the world: most major collections have at least one. Interestingly, many of these mandolinos are in more or less their original state of construction, probably because their design and small dimensions are not really suitable for conversion to later styles, as so many of the larger instruments were. Lute makers, for example, find it very difficult to find lutes in their original state on which to base their work, whereas it is very easy to locate totally original mandolinos.

I shall only point out a few representative instruments here, but the beginnings of a good list is published in Ernst Pohlmann's *Laute, Theorbe, Chitarrone* (Bremen, 1975, 369–79) under the anachronistic heading 'Pandurinen'. Various early instruments have already been mentioned in Chapter 1; the excellent seventeenth-century Matteo Sellas instrument was cited in Chapter 2; and the Giuseppe Fontanelli instruments were singled out in Chapter 3. Additional eighteenth-century instruments for makers to consider copying are those by: Benedetto Sanbretto, Rome, 1726 (Toronto, Royal Ontario Museum, no. 908.13.2) and Giovanni Smorsone, Rome, 1736 (Berlin, Musikinstrumenten-Museum, no. 5005) (see Illustration 4). There are other Smorsone instruments in Copenhagen, Claudius Musikhistoriske

Samling (no. 88); Milan, Castello Sforzesco (no. 209); and Hamburg, Museum für Hamburgishe Geschichte (no. 385). Another fine instrument is by Domenico Brambilla, Milan, 1768 (Berlin, Musikinstrumenten-Museum, no. 4668) (see Illustration 4), and a second instrument by him (1759) is in Ann Arbor (University of Michigan, no. 1049). An excellent example is by Fedele Barnia, Venice, 1767 (Kilmarnock, Van Raalte Collection, no. 41); another Barnia instrument of 1765 is in Berkeley (University of California).

These are just a few suggested examples, but there are many more mandolinos to be found in the collections in Washington DC (Smithsonian Institute), Milan (Castello Sforzesco), London (Victoria and Albert Museum), and New York (Metropolitan Museum of Art).

Useful Addresses

Modern lute makers are beginning to make reproductions of original mandolinos, though, of course, the revival of the instrument has only just begun and the demand is, as yet, modest. Various lute makers advertise in the specialist journals listed further along. There are a few hundred lute makers in America, England, and Europe, and only a few can be mentioned here:

Journals:

Early Music
Oxford University Press
7–8 Hatherley Street
London SW1P 2QT
Britain

Lute Society Journal
103 London Road
Oldham
Lancashire OL1 4BW
Britain

Journal of the Lute Society of America
PO Box 1327
Lexington, Virginia 24450
United States

Instrument Makers:
West Dean Crafts,
Musical Instrument Department (under the direction of Roger Rose),
West Dean, Nr. Chichester,
W. Sussex PO18 OQZ
Britain

Peter Forrester   H. E. Snyder
Beechwood Avenue   17 Vineland Drive
Aylmerton, Norfolk NR11 8QQ   Barrington, Rhode Island 02806
Britain   United States

Robert Lundberg
6532 Southeast 71st Avenue
Portland, Oregon 97206
United States

Gut and Pyramid strings can be obtained from most lute makers, or from:

Northern Renaissance Instruments   Donna Curry's Music
6 Needham Avenue   1780 Ft. Union Drive
Chorlton   Santa Fe
Manchester M21 2AA   New Mexico 87501
Britain   United States

Barton Catlines
34 Newberry Street
Sommerville, Massachusetts 02144
United States

Facsimiles and editions can be obtained through;

Brian Jordan Books   Boulder Early Music Shop
12 Green Street   2010 Fourteenth Street
Cambridge CB2 3JU   Boulder, Colorado 80302
Britain   United States

OMI   (Also strings)
PO Box 6019
FDR Station
New York, NY 10150
United States

5

Other Instruments Related to the Mandolino

The Soprano Lute

The soprano lute is a small but fully proportionate Renaissance lute used in the late sixteenth and the beginning of the seventeenth century. It is a rarely encountered instrument, usually having six or more courses which are meant to be tuned to the standard lute intervals of a 4th, a 4th, a major 3rd, a 4th, a 4th.

Praetorius (1619, 51) gives a chart for the relative tunings of the lute family from the highest-pitched member to the double bass, providing the specific pitch of the first (highest) of the six courses on each lute. His highest instrument is called the 'kleinen Octavlaute', for which he gives d″, or a tone lower, c″, as the first course. This means that his highest-pitched instrument is tuned either d″, a′, e′, c′, g, d or c″, g′, d′, b♭, f, c. It should be noted that Praetorius does not include the mandürichen (pandurina) among the lutes, but discusses it elsewhere as a separate instrument. The ordinary g′ lute, called the 'Recht Chorist, oder Alt Laute' by Praetorius, is the fourth member of the lute family described by him. His highest-pitched lute at d″ has the same tuning as the treble viol, and was used as the soprano voice of a consort of lutes. It was played in the same manner as the other lutes.

There are at least two surviving instruments which are the correct size for the tuning of Praetorius's smallest lute. They are both in the instrument collection of the Vienna Kunsthistorisches Museum (nos. C39 and C40) and are both by Wendelin Tieffenbrucker (or Wendelio Venere; see Harwood 1985). They are very much alike and both have seven courses, the first single, the rest double. The vibrating string length of the first is 44.2 cm and that of the second is 44 cm (Pohlmann 1975, 314; Schlosser 1920, 55 and plate 6). The instruments were made *c.*1600.

The soprano lute seems to have disappeared from use before the middle of the seventeenth century, except in Spain where it was used in the eighteenth century and called a *vandola*.

Vandola

The name of this type of soprano lute, vandola, was probably derived from 'mandola'. The earliest reference to the vandola is found in the 'Tractat breu', a supplement added anonymously to Joan Carles Amat's *Guitarra Espanola . . .* (Gerona, Francisco Oliva, n.d.) published sometime between 1703 and 1713.[1] A six-course instrument is described, and the writer mentions that four- and five-course examples are not common at this time. The tuning is discussed, and the writer also implies that the vandola can play from the chord symbols of the Spanish guitar.

The instrument is also discussed in Pablo Minguet y Yrol's *Reglas, y advertencias generales para tañer la guitarra, tiple, y vandola* (Madrid, n.d.) of *c.*1752. Minguet borrows from the 'Tractat breu', but also includes a picture of the vandola in his frontispiece.[2] This instrument has six double courses on its lute-shaped body and a flat, guitar-type pegboard. The vandola is also briefly discussed in Andrés de Sotos's *Arte para aprender . . . la guitarra* (Madrid, 1764).

All three sources, including the later editions of Amat, imply finger-style playing, and all agree that the tuning of the instrument is the same as for the soprano lute described above: d″, a′, e′, c′, g, d. No music specifically for the vandola survives.

The Large Mandola

Larger-sized mandolas are sometimes seen in seventeenth- and eighteenth-century pictures, such as those by Evaristo Baschenis (1617–77) (Rosci 1971,

[1] See Monica Hall's introduction to the facsimile of the *c.*1761 edition (Monaco, Editions Chanterelle S. A., 1980), p. ii.

[2] See the facsimile of Minguet y Yrol published by Minkoff Reprint (Geneva, 1984). The frontispiece is also reproduced in Tyler 1980, 113. The six-course vandola is the second from the left in the bottom row.

71–2, 77–8, etc.), and, as discussed fully in Chapter 2, Stradivari seems to have used the term mandola for an instrument larger than the mandolino. Indeed, one of Stradivari's instruments, his 'mandola granda' (no. 403) would probably have had a string length of about 60 cm.

Praetorius (1619, 28 and 53) gives tunings for lower-pitched instruments, two for a five-course instrument: c″, g′, c′, g, c and c″, f′, c′, f, c; and one for a four-course instrument: d″, g′, d′, g (Tyler 1981a, 23). These are the interval patterns of the French mandore, and one occasionally sees French pictures showing mandores larger than the ones suitable for a higher-pitched tuning.[3]

The Englishman James Talbot, in his manuscript notes on instruments from the end of the seventeenth century, discusses the term 'mandole'. He quotes his informant, 'Mr. Lewis', as saying: 'Mandole properly 5 courses/ranks whereof the lowest double the rest single'. He then gives the tuning in staff notation for a high-pitched 'mandole' of five courses: g″, d″, a′, f′, c′—the type of tuning found in a section of the Skene mandore manuscript of *c.*1630–50, and in the pieces by Filippo Sauli, discussed in Chapter 3. He then goes on to give a lower-pitched tuning for a larger six-course 'mandole': c″, g′, d′, b♭, f, c (Tyler 1981a, 27–8 and 30). These are the same pitches given by Praetorius for the alternate tuning of his kleinen Octavlaute. It should be noted that this second, lower tuning uses the intervals of a soprano lute previously discussed in this chapter. The six-course instrument measured by Talbot has a string length of 43 cm. Just such an instrument might be the one pictured on the title-page of Henry Playford's *Deliciae Musicae* (London, 1696).[4]

There is very little information as to the use of these larger instruments, but it seems likely that, in Italy, those with string lengths of about 55–65 cm were tuned to the intervals and pitches of the later six-string guitar. By the late eighteenth century, the Italian instrument was known as the *liuto*, and it is probably this instrument with its lute body, longish guitar-like neck and tuning, and sickle-shaped peg-box that Giovanni Francesco Giuliani intended for his lute parts in the mandolino quartets discussed in Chapter 3.[5]

---

[3] See Gill 1984, 605 for a painting *c.*1630 by Baugin.

[4] See Gill 1984, 604–5 for further stringing details of the Talbot instruments and for a reproduction of the Playford picture.

[5] The tuning arrangement is deduced from Giuliani's lute parts, which are mainly written in the bass clef but have occasional solo passages which are notated in the treble clef. As an instrument which

Mandora

This term is rarely, if ever, encountered in the sixteenth and seventeenth centuries. When it is encountered in the eighteenth century, it usually refers to a type of large bass lute used in German-speaking countries where it is also commonly known as a gallichone (or several other variants of this term!). The mandora or gallichone was used both as a solo and as a continuo instrument, and has a sizable repertory in tablature and in staff notation in the bass clef. Most of the repertory requires a tuning of d', a, f, c, G, F (sixth-course tunings vary), and, by 1790, Albrechtsberger gives a tuning identical to that of the modern guitar (plus two extra courses). Like the late Italian liuto, mentioned above, the mandora could also be played from the treble clef sounding an octave lower. An early nineteenth-century example of this is the accompaniment to an Italian 'canzoneta' by Domenico Dragonetti entitled 'Senza costrutto ho cara' (GB:Lbl Add. 17830, fos. 64–5). It is written in the treble clef in the arpeggio style and looks every bit like a typical classical guitar part, but the accompaniment is labelled 'mandora'.[6]

Bandurria/Bandurra

The Spanish bandurria seems to have originated as a small plucked instrument with a round back (see Bermudo's information quoted in Chapter 1). Little is known of it in the seventeenth century, but by the eighteenth century it seems to have become a flat-backed instrument with five double courses tuned in fourths. A brief tutor for this kind of instrument is Pablo Minguet y Yrol's *Reglas, y advertencios generales para tañer la bandurria . . .* (Madrid, n.d.) of *c.*1752. Minguet gives a picture of the instrument in a tuning chart on fo. 5 and on the frontispiece usually found in his entire series

plays in the bass range is unlikely to be able to play treble clef passages at written pitch, these treble clef passages must sound an octave lower than notated. These passages also have a number of chords in configurations which are identical to those of the six-string guitar. It therefore seems likely that Giuliani's lute is tuned like a modern guitar and reads the treble clef passages in the same manner as the modern guitar. See also the information on mandora.

[6] For a discussion of the gallichone (mandora) and its music, see the article 'Colascione' by Donald Gill in *New Grove Dictionary of Musical Instruments* (1984) 1: 434–6.

of little tutors.[7] It has a body outline which resembles somewhat an English guittar.[8] Like that instrument, it has a flat back. We are told by Minguet that the instrument uses gut strings and his picture also shows a plectrum. Of interest to us is the tuning he gives: a'', e'', b', f♯′, c♯′. It is entirely in fourths and tuned one tone higher than the mandolino.

Though there is no surviving Spanish music for the bandurria from this period (aside from Minguet's examples), there is a piece for it in a recently discovered Portuguese manuscript.[9] This is a five-course guitar manuscript now found in the library of the Gulbenkian Foundation in Lisbon (no shelf number), which contains music by various musicians associated with the Portuguese court of c.1720–50. On fos. 49–50ᵛ is a long piece entitled 'Battalla de Bandurra 5° ton.'; the composer is 'Botasella'. The sections of the piece are headed 'Entrada', 'Pointe a Cavalo', 'Passo', 'Clarim', 'Trombeteiro', and 'Bulha'. The piece is notated in five-line Italian tablature for an instrument of five courses. No pitches are given, but we can probably assume those given by Minguet to be correct. There are many chords in the tablature with configurations which, despite Minguet's implication of plectrum-playing, suggest that the Portuguese bandurra intended for this music was played finger-style, like an Italian mandolino.

[7] For Minguet's frontispiece, see Tyler 1980, 113. See also Ch. 5, n. 2.
[8] For a history of the English guittar, see Philip Coggin, ' " This Easy and Agreable Instrument", A History of the English Guittar' in *Early Music*, 15 (1987), 205–18.
[9] I am indebted to Manuel Morais for bringing this manuscript to my attention.

Appendix I

List of Primary Music Sources for the Mandolino

This list is divided into manuscripts and printed books which all contain music for solo mandolino, mandolino(s) in chamber music combinations, and mandolino(s) in concertos to *c*.1800. The list does not include mandolino parts in operas, oratorios, etc. as these are cited in Chapters 2 and 3. The list uses the standard location symbols established by RISM (*Répertoire International des Sources Musicales*, Munich, 1960–). For example: GB:Lbl = Great Britain: London, British Library. The RISM sigla are set forth in a separate listing which follows this explanation.

In some cases I have not been able to trace certain details, such as a shelf number, for a particular item; this will be indicated by a question mark in parenthesis. Wherever possible the original spellings in the manuscripts are used. The *circa* dates given are my own estimates if none are indicated in the original sources. Composers associated with each manuscript are listed next, and, in addition, the names of manuscript owners or players in parenthesis. These are followed by any pertinent remarks on the item, or a reference for further information. In the Vienna collection, though an individual item could possibly be intended for the Neapolitan mandoline, for the sake of completeness, the entire collection is itemized here. The present list corrects Zuth 1931.

This is the first complete bibliography of music sources for the mandolino to be published, though, hopefully, further research will uncover new items in the future.

Rism Sigla

A—AUSTRIA

A:Wgm   Vienna, Gesellschaft der Musikfreunde.
A:Wmi   Vienna, Musikwissenschaftliches Institut der Universität.

A:Wn   Vienna, Österreichische Nationalbibliothek,
            Musiksammlung.
A:Wst   Vienna, Stadtbibliothek, Musiksammlung.

B—BELGIUM

B:Bc   Brussels, Conservatoire Royal De Musique, Bibliothèque.

CS–ČSSR—CZECHOSLOVAKIA

CS-ČSSR:Pu Prague, Státní knihovna ČSR, Universitní knihovna,
            hudební oddelení.

D-brd—BUNDESREPUBLIK DEUTSCHLAND (WEST GERMANY)

D-brd:B   Berlin, Staatsbibliothek (Stiftung Preussischer
            Kulturbesitz).
D-brd:Hs   Hamburg, Staats-und Universitätsbibliothek,
            Musikabteilung.
D-brd:MÜd   Münster (Westfalen), Bischöfliches Diözesanarchiv.

D-ddr—DEUTSCHE DEMOKRATISCHE REPUBLIK
(EAST GERMANY)

D-ddr:Bds   Berlin, Deutsche Staatsbibliothek, Musikabteilung.
D-ddr:Dlb   Dresden, Sächsische Landesbibliothek, Musikabteilung.
D-ddr:SWL   Schwerin, Wissenschaftliche Allgemeinbibliothek
            (Landesbibliothek).

F—FRANCE

F:Pc   Paris, Bibliothèque Nationale (Fonds. Conservatoire).
F:Pn   Paris, Bibliothèque Nationale.

GB—GREAT BRITAIN

GB:Ckc   Cambridge, Kings College, Rowe Music Library.
GB:Ge   Glasgow, Euing Music Library.
GB:Lbl   London, The British Library.
GB:Lspencer London, private library of Robert Spencer.

I—ITALY

I:Ac	Assisi, Biblioteca comunale (now in I:Asf Assisi, Convento di San Francesco, Biblioteca)
I:Bc	Bologna, Civico Museo Bibliografico Musicale.
I:Fc	Florence, Biblioteca del Conservatorio di Musica 'L. Cherubini'.
I:Fn	Florence, Biblioteca Nazionale Centrale.
I:Ffornaciari	Florence, private library of Maestro M. Fornaciari.
I:Gi(l)	Genova, Biblioteca dell'Istituto (Liceo) Musicale 'Paganini'.
I:Ls	Lucca, Biblioteca del seminario arcivescovile presso la Curia.
I:Mc	Milan, Biblioteca del Conservatorio 'Giuseppe Verdi'.
I:MTventuri	Montecatini-Terme, private library of Antonio Venturi (now in I:MTc Montecatini-Terme, Biblioteca civica)
I:Tn	Turin, Biblioteca nazionale universitaria.
I:Vnm	Venice, Biblioteca nazionale Marciana.

P—PORTUGAL

P:Lgulbenkian	Lisbon, Library of the Gulbenkian Foundation.

US—UNITED STATES

US:AA	Ann Arbor, University of Michigan, Music Library.
US:Cn	Chicago, Newberry Library.
US:Wc	Washington DC, Library of Congress, Music Division.

MANUSCRIPT COLLECTIONS

Location: A:Wgm

SHELF NO.	TITLE	DATE	COMPOSER	REMARKS
19667/E	Sonata per Mandolino e Basso	c.1799	[Johann Conrad] Schlik	Zuth (1931, 93)
X19757/E	Sonata per Mandolino e Basso	c.1799	Giuseppe Blesber	Ibid. 92
X19758/E	Sonata per Mandolino e Basso	c.1799	Melchior Chiesa	Ibid. 92

SHELF NO.	TITLE	DATE	COMPOSER	REMARKS
X19759/E	Trio a Mandolino, Violino, e Violoncelle	*c*.1799	Dolphin	Ibid. 92
X19761/E	Sonata a Mandolino e Basso	*c*.1799	[Georg] Druschetzky	Ibid. 92
X19761 (Q16845)	VI Quartetti per Mandolino, Violino e Violoncello ò Viola e Liuto	*c*.1799	Giovanni Francesco Giuliani	Ibid. 90; for Neapolitan mandoline
19762/E.1	Divertimento a Mandolino, Violino e Basso [in C]	*c*.1799	Giovanni Hoffmann	Zuth (1931, 91)
19762/E.2	Divertimento a Mandolino, Violino e Basso [in G]	*c*.1799	Giovanni Hoffmann	Ibid. 91
19762/E.3	Divertimento a Mandolino, Violino e Basso [in C]	*c*.1799	Giovanni Hoffmann	Ibid. 91
19762/E.4	Divertimento a Mandolino, Violino e Basso [in D]	*c*.1799	Giovanni Hoffmann	Ibid. 91–2
19763/3	Sonata a Due Mandolini	*c*.1799	Giovanni Hoffmann	Ibid. 93
19763/4	Sonata a Due Mandolini	*c*.1799	Giovanni Hoffmann	Ibid. 93
19763/5	Sonata in G a Mandolino e Basso	*c*.1799	Giovanni Hoffmann	Ibid. 92
19763/E.1	Sonata a Mandolino e Basso	*c*.1799	Giovanni Hoffmann	Ibid. 93
19763/E.2	Sonata a Mandolino e Basso	*c*.1799	Giovanni Hoffmann	Ibid. 93
19764/E.1	Quartetto a Mandolino, Violino, Viola e Basso	*c*.1799	Giovanni Hoffmann	Ibid. 91
19764/E.2	Quartetto in A a Mandolino, Violino, Viola	*c*.1799	Giovanni Hoffmann	Ibid. 91
19765/E	Cassazione in G a Mandolino Primo, Mandolino Secondo, e Violoncelle	*c*.1799	Giovanni Hoffmann	Ibid. 91; cello part only
X19766/E	Concerto a Mandolino Principale, Due Violini, Viola, Oboe, Corni e Basso	*c*.1799	Giovanni Hoffmann	Ibid. 90
X19844/D	Sonata in C a Mandolino e Basso	*c*.1799	Giuseppe Blesber	Ibid. 92
X23531/f	Serenada in D a Mandolino e Viola	*c*.1799	Giovanni Hoffmann	Ibid. 93
X47299	Sonata per Due Mandolini	*c*.1799	Kistner	Ibid. 93
X47300	3 Poloness a Mandolino e Basso	*c*.1799	Anon.	Ibid. 92
X47301	Sonata in G a Mandolino e Basso	*c*.1799	Anon.	Ibid. 92
X47302	Galanterie a Mandolino e Basso	*c*.1799	Anon.	Ibid. 92
X47303	Sonata a Mandolino e Basso	*c*.1799	Anon.	Ibid. 92

SHELF NO.	TITLE	DATE	COMPOSER	REMARKS
X47304	Sonata per Mandolino e Basso	*c.*1799	Anon.	Ibid. 92
X47305	Duetto in C a Mandolino Primo e Mandolino Secondo	*c.*1799	Anon.	Ibid. 93
X47306	Duetto per Due Mandolini	*c.*1799	Anon.	Ibid. 93
X49843/a	Quartetto a Mandolino, Violino, Viola e Basso	*c.*1799	Anon.	Ibid. 91
X49843/b	Quartetto in D a Mandolino, Violino, Viola e Basso	*c.*1799	Anon.	Ibid. 91
X49844	Divertimento in D a Mandolino Primo, Mandolino Secondo e Basso	*c.*1799	Anon.	Ibid. 91
X56283	Mandolino	*c.*1799	Anon.	Ibid. 93; partbook with 6 mvts.
X56.284	Mandolino	*c.*1799	Anon.	Ibid. 93; mandolino part for 3-mvt. piece
X56.285	Mandolino	*c.*1799	Anon.	Ibid. 93; not for mandolino; 7 pieces for guitar
(?)	Concerto in G a Mandolino Principale, due Violini, due Oboe, due Corni, Viola e Basso	*c.*1799	Anon. [Hoffmann?]	Ibid. 90; now missing from library

Location: A:Wn

MS. Mus. 1082	Pour les Cistre	*c.*1765	Anon.	

Location: CS-ČSSR:Pu

II KK 36	Sonata al Mandolino solo & Basso	*c.*1710	Francesco Contini	Wolf (1919, 123–4); Boetticher (1978, 315); all these items from CS-ČSSR:Pu are in French tablature
Ibid.	Partita per C. C. . . . per il Mandolino	*c.*1710	Filippo Sauli	
Ibid.	Partita	*c.*1710	Filippo Sauli	
Ibid.	[Partita]	*c.*1710	Anon.	
Ibid.	[Partita]	*c.*1710	Anon.	
Ibid.	Partita per g sol re ut	*c.*1710	Filippo Sauli	
Ibid.	Partita	*c.*1710	Filippo Sauli	

Location: D-brd:B

SHELF NO.	TITLE	DATE	COMPOSER	REMARKS
Mus. ms 30135	6 notturni a 2 mandolini e basso	*c.*1790	Ignazio Greggio	

Location: D-brd:MÜd[1]

Sant. Hs. 3424	2 Sinfonie a Mandolino Solo	*c.*1730	[Nicola] Romaldi	
Sant. Hs. 3448	Libro di Sonate per il Mandolino	*c.*1750	(Bartolomeo Ruspoli) Caldara, Valentini	121 separate short pieces in 4-line Italian tablature
Sant. Hs. 4014	Concerto in A per Mandolla	*c.*1740	Cristoforo Signorelli	with 2 violins and b.c.
Sant. Hs. 4015	Concerto in C per Mandolla	*c.*1740	Cristoforo Signorelli	with 2 violins and b.c.
Sant. Hs. 4016	Concerto in C per Mandolla	*c.*1740	Cristoforo Signorelli	with 2 violins and b.c.
Sant. Hs. 4017	Concerto in A per Mandolla	*c.*1740	Cristoforo Signorelli	with 2 violins and b.c.
Sant. Hs. 4018	Sonate a due Mandolle solo in G	*c.*1740	Cristoforo Signorelli	
Sant. Hs. 4019	Sonate a due Mandolle solo del Signorelli in C	*c.*1740	Cristoforo Signorelli	
Sant. Hs. 4020	Sonate per la Mandolla in G	*c.*1740	Cristoforo Signorelli	
Sant. Hs. 4021	Sonate per la Mandolla del Cristofaro Signorelli in D	*c.*1740	Cristofaro Signorelli	
Sant. Hs. 4022	Sonate per la Mandolla in G	*c.*1740	Cristoforo Signorelli	
Sant. Hs. 4107	[Untitled]	*c.*1730	Anon.	4-line Italian tablature; 64 fos. of vocal and instrumental items
Sant. Hs. 4108	[Untitled]	*c.*1730	Valentini	4-line Italian tablature; 36 fos.
Sant. Hs. 4109	[Untitled]	*c.*1730	Anon.	4-line Italian tablature; 16 fos.
Sant. Hs. 4110	[Untitled]	*c.*1730	Anon.	4-line Italian tablature; 23 fos.

[1] I would like to thank Stephen Morey for his generosity in communicating to me his discovery of the full extent of the MÜd manuscripts just in time for them to be included in this list. Most of the manuscripts seem to have once been the property of 'Don Bartolomeo Ruspoli, Principe di Ceuestra'. The possible connection between these manuscripts and the music-making at the Roman court of Francesco Ruspoli, patron of Handel, Alessandro Scarlatti, Antonio Caldara, and Giuseppe Valentini make them highly interesting and potentially important.

SHELF NO.	TITLE	DATE	COMPOSER	REMARKS
Sant. Hs. 4111	[Untitled]	*c.*1730	Anon.	4-line Italian tablature; 5 fos.
Sant. Hs. 4112	[Untitled]	*c.*1730	Anon.	4-line Italian tablature; 32 fos.

Location: D-ddr:Bds

Landsberg 313/8	Concerto con Mandolino obligato	*c.*1740	Johann Adolf Hasse	Drummond (1980, 251)

Location: D-ddr:Dlb

2389/o/4 no. 1	Concerto con Due Flauti, due Tiorbe, due Mandolini, due Salmo, due Violini in Tromba Marina et un Violoncello	*c.*1740	Antonio Vivaldi	Ryom (1986, RV558)

Location: D-ddr:SWL

5799	Mandolino Solo [G]	*c.*1780	Zaneboni	3-mvt. sonata for mandolino and basso
5800	Mandolino Solo[B♭]	*c.*1780	Zaneboni	3-mvt. sonata for mandolino and basso
5801	Mandolino Solo [C]	*c.*1780	Zaneboni	3-mvt. sonata for mandolino and basso; this and the other Zaneboni pieces may be attempts at adapting for some other type of mandolin

Location: F:Pn

Rés. Vmb ms. 9	Libro per la Mandola	1703	(Matteo Caccini), Pietro Paolo Cappelini, Niccolò Ceccherini, Federico Meccoli	

Location: GB:Lspencer

(?)	Sei Sonate a due Mandolini e Basso	*c.*1800	Giovanni Francesco Giuliani	'Basso o Liuto' partbook only
(?)	(no title)	1698	(Domenico Veterani)	6 mandolino pieces in a guitar MS; Italian tablature

Location: I:Ac

SHELF NO.	TITLE	DATE	COMPOSER	REMARKS
N. 17/2	Sonata a Mandolino e Basso	1769	F. Giuseppe Paolucci	Sartori (1962, 312)
N. 178/1	Sonata a due Mandolini e Basso [G]	1758	F. Giuseppe Paolucci	Ibid.
Ibid.	Sonata a due Mandolini e Basso [Cm]	1758	F. Giuseppe Paolucci	Ibid.
Ibid.	Sonata a due Mandolini e Basso [G]	c.1758–69	F. Giuseppe Paolucci	Ibid.
Ibid.	Sonata a due Mandolini e Basso [C]	c.1758–69	F. Giuseppe Paolucci	Ibid.
Ibid.	Sonata a due Mandolini e Basso [G]	1759	F. Giuseppe Paolucci	Ibid.
Ibid.	Sonata a due Mandolini e Basso [Bm]	1759	F. Giuseppe Paolucci	Ibid.
Ibid.	Sonata a due Mandolini e Basso [G]	?1761	F. Giuseppe Paolucci	Ibid.
Ibid.	Sonata a due Mandolini e Basso [F]	?1761	F. Giuseppe Paolucci	Ibid.
Ibid.	Sonata a due Mandolini e Basso [D]	1761	F. Giuseppe Paolucci	Ibid.
Ibid.	Sonata a due Mandolini e Basso [G]	?1761	F. Giuseppe Paolucci	Ibid.
Ibid.	Sonata a due Mandolini e Basso [G]	?1761	F. Giuseppe Paolucci	Ibid.
Ibid.	Sonata a due Mandolini e Basso [G]	?1761	F. Giuseppe Paolucci	Ibid.

Location: I:Bc

SHELF NO.	TITLE	DATE	COMPOSER	REMARKS
EE 155	Suonate à Mandolino, è Arcileuto	c.1759–60	Antonio Tinazzoli	Cristoforetti (1984); these items from I:Bc for mando-lino are found in the Dalla Casa MS for arcileuto francese
Ibid.	Concerto à Mandolino, è Basso del Arcileuto	c.1759–60	Giuseppe Vaccari	
Ibid.	Concerto à Mandolino, è Basso del Arcileuto	c.1759–60	Giuseppe Vaccari	
Ibid.	Concerto à Mandolino, è Basso del Arcileuto	c.1759–60	Lodovico Fontanelli	
Ibid.	Sonta . . . à Mandola è Basso del Arcileuto	c.1759–60	Anon.	

Location: I:Fc

SHELF NO.	TITLE	DATE	COMPOSER	REMARKS
3802	Diverse arie di danza per mandola	c.1680	Anon.	Italian tablature

Location: I:Fn

SHELF NO.	TITLE	DATE	COMPOSER	REMARKS
Magl. xix 28	Sonate	*c.*1650–70	Anon.	Becherini (1959, 10–11); Boetticher (1978, 107); Italian tablature
Magl. xix 29	Sonate	*c.*1650–70	Agnolo Conti and Anon.	Becherini (1959, 11); Boetticher (1978, 108); Italian tablature

Location: I:Ffornaciari

(?)	Sonata per Armandolino	*c.*1750	G. B. Sammartini	Pitrelli (*c.*1983, II no. 48)
(?)	Sonata di Armandolino è Basso	*c.*1750	[Sammartini?]	Ibid. II no. 49
(?)	Sonata a Mandolino a Primo e Basso	*c.*1750	Anon.	Ibid. II no. 12
(?)	Sonata, a Primo e Basso	*c.*1750	Anon.	
(?)	Sonata	*c.*1750	Anon.	

Location: I:Gi(l)

SS.B.1.2. (H.8)	Duetto a due Amandolini	*c.*1790	Alessandro Rolla	Pintacuda (1966, 96)
SS.B.1.3 (H.8)	Duetto a due Amandolini	*c.*1790	Alessandro Rolla	

Location: I:Ls

B.254	VI Quartetti per due Mandolini, Viola, Liuto	?1799	G. F. Giuliani	Maggini (1965, 266); for Neapolitan mandoline?
Ibid.	VI Quartetti per due Mandolini, Flauto e Violoncello	?1799	G. F. Giuliani	Ibid.
Ibid.	VI Quartetti per due Mandolini, Flauto e Viola	?1799	G. F. Giuliani	Ibid.

Location: I:Mc

Noseda M 30.3	Sonata per Mandolino	*c.*1750	Gaetano Monza	Pitrelli (*c.*1983, II no. 4)
Noseda O 31.8	Sinfonia per la Mandòla	*c.*1750	Francesco Piccone	
Noseda O 31.9 [A]	Studio per la Mandola	*c.*1750	Francesco Piccone	
Noseda O 31.9 [B]	Pastorale	*c.*1750	(Piccone?)	
Noseda O 31.10	[Sonata]	*c.*1750	Francesco Piccone	
Noseda O 14.1	Sinfonia a due Mandole e Basso	*c.*1730	Nicola Romaldi	Ibid. III no. 8
Noseda P 34.13	Minuetto	*c.*1750	Bonaventura Terreni	Ibid. II no. 36; amandolino

SHELF NO.	TITLE	DATE	COMPOSER	REMARKS
Noseda P 34.14	Sonata	*c.*1750	Bonaventura Terreni	with cembalo accompaniment
Noseda Z 18.36	Sonata per li Mandolini	*c.*1750	Anon	

Location: I:Tn

Giordano 28	Concerto per Mandolino	*c.*1730–40	Antonio Vivaldi	Ryom (1986, RV425)
	Concerto per 2 Mandolini	*c.*1730–40	Antonio Vivaldi	Ibid. RV532

Location: I:Vmc

B. 124–149 N. 142	Suonata per Mandolino e Basso	*c.*1750	Skawronsky	

Location: I:Vnm

IV COD. cccclxxvi	Per Mandolino. Suonatine	*c.*1750	Girolamo Venier	Pitrelli (*c.*1983, II nos. 5–11); 7 pieces in the treble and bass clefs
(?)	Arie per il Mandolino	1720	Anon.	

Location: P:Lgulbenkian

(?)	(Guitar MS; no title)	*c.*1720	Bottasella	one piece for 'Bandurra' in guitar MS; Italian tablature

Location: US:Cn

Case 3A 17	Principii per imparare . . . Scala per l'Amandolino	*c.*1800	Anon.	dance pieces for two instruments

Location: US:Wc

M295A (case)	2 Sonate per Mandolino e Basso	*c.*1740	[Carlo Arrigoni?]	
M374.A76 (case)	Concerto per Mandolino, 2 Violini, Viola, e Basso	*c.*1740	Carlo Arrigoni	
M374.A77 (case)	Sonata Trio per Mandolino, Violino, e Basso	*c.*1740	[Carlo Arrigoni?]	
M23.5965 (case)	Sonata di Mandolino [Dm]		G. P. Sesto da Trento	for mandolino and basso
M23.5966 (case)	Suonata [C]		N. Susier	for mandolino and basso

PUBLISHED MUSIC

COMPOSER	TITLE	LOCATION	DATE
Giuseppe Gaetano Boni	*Divertimenti per camera a violino, violone, cimbalo, flauto, e mandola*, Op. 2 (Rome, n.d.) (RISM B 3490), 12 sonatas	I:Bc	*c.*1725
Gasparo Cantarelli	*Sonate Nuove di Mandola*, 2 balletti, on p. 49 of G. P. Ricci, *Scuola d'intavolatura . . . la chitarriglia Spagnuola* (Rome, 1677)(RISM BVI² II: 702)	F:Pn; GB:Lbl	1677
[Nicolas Cloes]	*One Hundred French Songs set for Voice, German Flute, Violin, Harpsichord and Pandola* (London, n.d.) (RISM C 3216)	D-brd:Hs; GB:Ckc; GB:Ge; GB:Lbl; US:Wc	(1749)
Willem De Fesch	*XX Canzonette a voce sola . . . potersi suonare con violino, flauto traversa, e mandolino* (London, n.d.) (RISM F 548)	B:Bc; GB:Lbl; US:AA; US:Wc	*c.*1730
Giovanni Hoffmann²	*Tre duetti per il mandolino, e violino*, Op. 1 (Vienna, n.d.) (RISM H 6249)	A:Wmi; A:Wst; GB:Lbl	(1799)

² Hoffmann's two 'duetti' collections were published in Vienna by Artaria & Co., and it is known that Op. 1 was republished in 1801 (Francesco Artaria) and in 1804 (Mollo). In 1804, Johann Traeg and Son (Vienna) listed a volume of the 'Tre duetti' (Op. 1?) in their catalogue (*Erster Nachtrag zu dem Verzeichniss alter und neuer sowohl geschriebener als gestochener Musikalien*, p. 31). Traeg listed both printed music (his own as well as that of other publishers) and manuscript copies of a huge range of items. The 1804 catalogue also offers a Hoffmann concerto which was probably in manuscript. A 1799 Traeg catalogue (*Verzeichnisse alter und neuer sowohl geschriebener als gestochener Musikalien*) offers the following items by Hoffmann: a 'Trio p. il Mand. e B.'; three 'Serenatas' for mandolino and viola (in C, F, and D); a 'Cassazione p. il Mand. V. Viola e Vllo'; two quartets for the same combination in D and A; and a 'trio à Mand. Viola e B.'. These are apparently all in manuscript as there is no evidence that any of them were ever printed. Traeg also offers several anonymous mandolino items and a sonata for 'Mandolino e Basso' by Schlik. Looking at the similar list of manuscripts in the A:Wgm collection, it seems likely that the Vienna manuscripts came from the firm of Johann Traeg in *c.*1799.

COMPOSER	TITLE	LOCATION	DATE
Giovanni Hoffmann (see n. 2)	*Tre duetti per il mandolino, e violino,* Op. 2 (Vienna, n.d.)	Lost. See Ernst Ludwig Gerber, *Neues Historisch-Biographisches Lexicon der Tonkünstler* (Leipzig, 1812–14; repr. 1966, 702)	(1799)
Robert Valentine	*Sonate per il flauto traversiero, col basso che possono servire per violino, et oboe,* Op. 12 (Rome, n.d.) (RISM V 80) Another edn.: (Paris, n.d.) (RISM V 81)	GB:Lbl B:Bc; F:Pc; F:Pn	(1730)

Appendix II

Music Examples

1. 'Bure' by Agniolo Conti: the earliest written source of mandolino music (*c*.1650–70).

2. 'Corrente', Anon.: an early example of the simple dance style (mostly single-line with a few sparse chords). The configuration of the second chord of measure 6 points to finger-style technique for the right hand. In Italian tablature, dots under specific notes usually indicate that the note is to be played with the right-hand index finger (which usually plays unstressed notes); but in this tablature, the dots probably indicate that the thumb is to be used since they are all under stressed notes.

3. 'Alemanda—Fuga' by Niccolò Ceccherini: an early example of music for mandolino/mandola in staff notation. The music is more extensive and sophisticated than the earlier dance style; finger-style technique seems to be required, as indicated in bars 15 and 16 of the Fuga.

4. 'Transit Aetas' by Antonio Vivaldi: a fine example of an aria with mandolino obbligato. The mandolino part provides an introductory section, interludes, and simultaneous interplay with the solo voice.

5. 'Sonata per Armandolino' by Giovanni Battista Sammartini: a recently discovered work which appears to be unknown in the standard studies and literature on Sammartini. A delightful example of the three-movement solo sonata with continuo accompaniment (here an un-figured bass), it is printed here complete for the first time.

'Bure' by Agniolo Conti

Sources: I:Fn Magl. xix 29, fo. 20ᵛ
          F:Pn Rés. Vmc ms. 6, fo. 1

'Corrente' by Anon.

(Transcription)

Source: I:Fc MS. 3802, fo. 3

'Alemanda—Fuga' by Niccolò Ceccherini

Alemanda

Fuga

(*continued*)

'Alemanda—Fuga' by Niccolò Ceccherini (*continued*)

Source: *Libro per la Mandola* (1703), F:Pn Rés. Vmb ms. 9, fos. 5–6

'Transit Aetas' by Antonio Vivaldi

(continued)

'Transit Aetas' by Antonio Vivaldi (*continued*)

Source: *Juditha Triumphans*, RV645 (1716) by Antonio Vivaldi

'Sonata per Armandolino' by Giovanni Battista Sammartini

(*continued*)

'Sonata per Armandolino' by Giovanni Battista Sammartini (*continued*)

(*continued*)

'Sonata per Armandolino' by Giovanni Battista Sammartini (*continued*)

(*continued*)

'Sonata per Armandolino' by Giovanni Battista Sammartini (*continued*)

Source: I:Ffornaciari

(1)

PART II

The Mandoline

by Paul Sparks

6

Naples and the Origins of a New Instrument

The entry of Charles Bourbon into Naples in 1734 at the head of his Spanish army signalled the beginning of a golden age of Neapolitan culture. Although Naples was the third largest city in Europe (after London and Paris), and the Neapolitan kingdom comprised the whole of the south of Italy (including Sicily), the region had languished under foreign rule for centuries until Charles established an autonomous kingdom and encouraged the emergence of a distinctive Neapolitan style in art and music. The next few years saw the building of the San Carlo opera house, the porcelain factory at Capodimonte, and the enlargement of the Palazzo Reale, while increased artistic patronage led to a flowering of Neapolitan painting.[1]

In music, a distinctive Neapolitan style was developing, lighter and more melodic than that found elsewhere in Europe. G. B. Pergolesi is today the best remembered of a school of composers who developed a form of opera in Neapolitan dialect. The four Neapolitan conservatories became famous throughout Europe and a period of study at one of them was an important step in the career of any aspiring operatic musician. Throughout the eighteenth century, Naples exported a steady stream of composers and singers to other European capitals, and the Neapolitan style became a principal influence on international taste.

Naples has had a long association with a variety of popular plectrum instruments, dating back to at least the fifteenth century, when Arabian wire-strung long lutes of the bouzouki type were introduced there, were modified with characteristics of Italian lute construction, and became known as the colascione.[2] Metal strung guitars were popular in Naples, often strummed with a plectrum as an accompaniment to song and dance (Baines

---

[1] R. B. Litchfield (1981) gives an excellent historical summary of this period.

[2] This instrument is described in Ch. 10.

1966, 49). A third instrument is discussed by Filip Bonani in his *Gabinetto armonico* (1722) where he describes the pandora:

> The Neapolitans call by this name an instrument slightly different in form to the mandola, but much bigger. It has eight metal strings which are struck with a plectrum, and it gives out a jangling sound.[3]

An important breakthrough in construction occurred in Naples *c.*1740 with the introduction of the canted table. Canting was accomplished by bending the wood over a hot poker just behind the bridge before fixing it to the body of the instrument; the final shape distributed the string tension more equally throughout the whole instrument than was the case with the traditional flat table. This new design became a common and distinctive Neapolitan trait, particularly on the chitarra battente[4] and the newly developed mandoline.

During the eighteenth century the emphasis on musical performance was transferred from the intimate surroundings of private houses to the larger spaces of the ever-increasing number of public concert halls and opera houses. Luthiers responded to this challenge by increasing the string tension, and often the size, of instruments so that they could survive in these larger surroundings. Some instruments, such as those of the viol family, were unable to make the change and never moved from domestic to public performance. In the case of the mandolin, Neapolitan luthiers deepened the bowl of the instrument and made use of the canted table in order that a greater string tension could be borne than was the case with the mandolino.

Instruments of this period commonly have tables made from fir or pine, with the back (or bowl) constructed from between eleven and thirty-five sycamore, rosewood, or maple ribs. On the best Neapolitan mandolines each rib was fluted (that is, scooped out after it was glued in place, so that the back presented a series of crests and troughs). The pair of ribs nearest the soundboard are much deeper than the others and give the mandoline its distinctive deep curve, much more pronounced than that encountered on any other type of plucked instrument. The hardwood fingerboard was decorated with ivory on the best instruments and lay flush with the soundboard, unlike

---

[3] The accompanying illustrations in Bonani's book are thoroughly unreliable—his artist's drawing of the pandora has 10 tuning pegs!

[4] Although earlier instruments with canted table exist, such as the chitarra battente by Jacobus Stadler, Munich 1624 (London, Hill Collection), these examples have clearly been modified after their original construction.

modern instruments where the fingerboard runs over the table and stops at the soundhole. Metal or ivory frets were fixed into slots in the fingerboard. The flat pegboard with sagittal pegs followed the Neapolitan tradition of guitar and chitarra battente construction rather then the scrolled head and side pegs of the mandolino. The soundhole was open and between it and the bridge was placed a protective plate made of either tortoiseshell or a piece of hard wood. By fixing the strings to hitch pins at the base, the problem of table rupture, which is encountered on the lute-type of fixed glued bridge at high tensions, was avoided. The overall length of the instrument was about 56 cm, with a string playing length of about 33.5 cm.

But the most significant distinction between mandoline and mandolino is not in construction but in tuning. The traditional fourth-based tuning of the mandolino, a tuning which favours a chordal style of playing, has been replaced by fifths which give the mandoline many characteristics of the violin. Whereas to a conventionally trained musician of the period the mandolino was a separate study, the mandoline was easily understood by any composer or performer familiar with the violin, which had become the undisputed king of the bowed-instrument family. As Signor Leoné of Naples pointed out on page 1 of his *Méthode* of 1768:

> The mandoline is tuned in fifths exactly like the violin; there are some other instruments of roughly the same shape which are called Mandoles in Italy, and which strangers often confuse with the one under discussion here, which is the most perfect and which ought justly to participate in the prerogatives of the violin, which is acknowledged to be the most universal and widely-used instrument.

mandolino   mandoline

Credit for the development of the mandoline is usually given to the Vinaccia family, although several other Neapolitan luthiers are known to have been making mandolines at about the same time.[5] The earliest surviving mandoline is a tenor instrument (mandola)[6] dated 1744, made by

---

[5] Apart from the Vinaccia family, the most important Neapolitan mandoline luthiers during the second half of the eighteenth century were Donatus Filano and the Fabricatore brothers.

[6] *Mandola* is used here in its modern sense as an instrument with four pairs of strings tuned either like a viola, or an octave below the mandoline. It has no connection with the mandola described in Chs. 2 and 3. See also Ch. 10.

Gaetano Vinaccia and now no. 3182 in the *Conservatoire royal de musique* in Brussels (Baines 1966). The earliest surviving mandoline proper dates from 1753 (Coates 1985, 136–9), but it is well documented that the instrument had become popular in Naples prior to this date.

In Naples, the mandoline was generally regarded as a 'popular' rather than a 'serious' instrument. A school of mandoline players and composers grew up there, but was never accepted into the conservatories. Giuseppe Giuliano was considered to be a leading exponent of the instrument, as Pietro Denis remarks on page 3 of his Paris *Méthode* of 1768: 'I have seen Mr Julien, whom I believe to be the finest player of the mandoline, in Naples . . .'.

Travellers to Naples mention that the instrument was popular at every level of society. Charles Burney, for example, in his *Musical Tour* (1771), noted in his diary for 23 October 1770:

The Second Week at Naples.
This evening in the street some genuine Neapolitan singing, accompanied by a caloscioncino, a mandoline, and a violin; I sent for the whole band upstairs, but, like other street music, it was best at a distance . . . (vol. 1, p. 254).

The instrument was widely written for by Neapolitan composers, occasionally in operas in Neapolitan dialect, but chiefly in instrumental music. However, many Neapolitan composers were making their livings abroad at this time, and one can learn more by looking at published and manuscript writings from other countries than from Italy itself. Of all the European centres of mandoline activity in this period by far the most important and thriving was Paris, where the instrument was to enjoy great popularity during the second half of the eighteenth century.

7

The Mandoline in France

The eighteenth century was for France a period of massive economic decline, with the French people becoming increasingly unwilling to foot the
bill for royal extravagance and for the disastrous series of wars in which the
country was engaged. By the end of the Seven Years War (1756–63) fought
against Britain and Prussia, France was virtually bankrupt.

But against this backdrop of national insolvency, the elegant life of the
titled and wealthy continued unabated, refusing to recognize the mounting
economic crisis in France. Art, and in particular music, was eagerly patron-
ized by the privileged strata of society. Opera thrived, as did instrumental
concerts, the most celebrated being the regular concerts of the *Concert
Spirituel* in Paris,[1] which were held on days of religious significance when
opera was considered unsuitable. This patronage encouraged singers and
musicians throughout Europe to try their fortune in Paris (and in Lyon
which was the second city of France), especially those from Italy, whose
lyrical musical style had become immensely popular in France, where it was
termed *style galant*.

Paradoxically, in the midst of such artificiality and cultivation, the ideal-
ized image of pastoral life was exalted by artists and thinkers alike. Rousseau, for example, praised the natural simplicity of *l'homme sauvage*, and at
Versailles the aristocracy dressed up as shepherds and shepherdesses and
serenaded each other with music played on pastoral instruments, such as the
vielle (hurdy-gurdy) and the musette (bagpipes).

In 1752 an Italian opera company created a sensation in Paris with performances of Pergolesi's *La Serva Padrona*. The light melodic style of this
Neapolitan *opera buffa* encouraged a taste amongst the French for Italian art
and music. Rousseau argued in favour of this style, stating that a musical
performance 'must at one time carry only one melody to the ear and one idea
to the soul', (Rousseau 1753, 275) and composed an opera of his own, *Le
Devin du Village*, to show how the new style could be applied to the French
language.

[1] Constant Pierre (1975) gives a full history of the *Concert*.

During the 1750s and 1760s France enjoyed an unprecedented influx of Neapolitan musicians, chiefly opera composers and singers who worked at both the Comédie Italienne and the *Opéra*. In their wake came many instrumentalists, including a number of mandolinists who earned their living as teachers, performers, and composers of music for their instrument.

The first professional mandolinist in Paris during this period is known to have been the Roman Carlo Sodi (or Sody), who performed there on 18 October 1749, and at a *concert spirituel* on 6 April 1750 (*Mercure de France*, December 1749, pt. 1: 201, and May 1750, 188). Sodi worked principally as a violinist at the Comédie Italienne and made no other recorded appearances as a mandolinist although he was the first recorded teacher of the instrument in Paris.[2] During the 1750s the colascione was being championed in Paris by Giacomo Merchi and his brother, both Neapolitans,[3] and it was not until the 1760s that the mandoline began to establish itself as the dominant Neapolitan instrument there.

The year 1760 marked the beginning of the mandoline's great popularity in Paris, due to the appearance of two leading players at the *Concert Spirituel*. At Easter, Giovanni Cifolelli performed there: 'Signor Cifotelli [sic], a musician of the Elector Palatin, played a mandoline sonata of his own composition. The mandoline is a sort of little guitar: and signor Cifotelli played it with every possible skill.'[4] Cifolelli subsequently settled in Paris, where he worked as a composer, mandolinist and singer. A fascinating description of his talents appeared on page 78 of the *Journal de Musique* in July 1770:

We have had in this city for some time a virtuoso whose talents deserve in every way to be universally known. M. Cifolelli, an Italian, has in his manner of singing all the graces which one admires in artists of his country, with none of their faults. . . . He adds to this merit that of accompanying himself most agreeably upon the mandoline, and of composing charming music.

---

[2] Jèze (1759) lists only Sodi as a *maître de mandoline*.

[3] They appeared at a *concert spirituel* in 1753 and gained an approving review in *Mercure de France* (June 1753, pt. 2: 163). On 13 June 1753 the Duc de Luynes also remarked favourably on their performance in his *Mémoires* (1860; rept. 1970). The brothers stayed in Paris and are listed in Jèze (1759) as *maîtres de colascione*. See also Ch. 10, 'Colascione'.

[4] *Mercure de France* June 1760, 237. Didier Le Roux (1986) states that the Elector Palatin was the sovereign of the small duchy of *Deux-Ponts*, near Luxembourg. Cifolelli's daughter became a celebrated *cantatrice* at the Comédie-Italienne, noted for her 'pleasing figure and slender, elegant waist' by the anonymous author of *Tablettes de Renommée* (1785).

The penning of this panegyric by the *Journal*'s editor, Nicolas Framery, may not be entirely unconnected to the fact that these two men had just collaborated on an *opéra comique*, 'L'Italienne', which was performed that year at the Comédie Italienne.

The second, and more important, appearance in 1760 was that of Signor Leoni (or Leoné) of Naples, who performed one of his own sonatas at the Pentecost *concert*, and appeared again on Corpus Christi where, according to *Mercure*: 'He played the mandoline with great skill' (*Mercure de France*, June 1760, 237; July 1760, pt. 1). Leoné appeared at a further four *concerts* in 1766, those on 8 September, and 8, 24, and 25 December, this time eliciting a most favourable review in *Mercure*:

8 December . . . M. Leoné executed a mandoline solo of a very good sort, and at the same time of pleasing taste. This artist's skill was astonishing and he was a genuine success, which was all the more flattering for him because his chosen instrument is not loud, compared to the size of the venue where he was displaying his talents. (*Mercure de France*, January 1767, pt. 1: 188–9.)

Leoné does not appear to have been resident in Paris, but was the *Maître de mandoline* in the household of the Duc de Chartres during the 1760s. A great deal of his mandoline music was published in Paris, commencing with the first known Parisian mandoline publication, *30 Variations* (1761), and including his *Méthode Raisonnée Pour passer du Violon à la Mandoline* (1768), the most detailed and important of all eighteenth-century tutors for the instrument. Leoné called himself simply 'Signor Leoni [or M. Leoné] de Naples'; his Christian name is uncertain.[5]

Paris was the centre of all music publishing during the eighteenth century, and composers from all over Europe had their works published there. As the market for published mandoline music was always relatively small compared to those for standard orchestral instruments, the works of mandolinists, such as Leoné's *Six Duo*, were usually described on the title-page as

[5] The 1983 Minkoff reprint of Leoné's *Méthode* gives his name as Pietro, but offers no explanation for this. Le Roux (1986) gives his name as Gabriele and considers the mandoline virtuoso and Gabriele Leone, a London music publisher during the 1760s, to be the same man. This is certainly possible, as Leoné is known to have been in London in 1766 (see Ch. 8, n., 4). Several manuscripts in the Fondo Noseda, I:Mc are entitled 'Duetto a due Mandolini del Sig^r. Gabriele Leoné. 1789'. However these are merely copies of Leoné's 1762 duets and, given the much later date on the manuscripts, I do not think that too much weight should be placed on them, considering that no Parisian source of the 1760s or 1770s ever offered a Christian name for Leoné.

Illustration 5*a*. Pierre Lacour le Père, 'Portrait of André-François-Benoit-Elisabeth Leberthon, vicomte de Virelade' (late eighteenth century).

Illustration 5*b*. Johann Heinrich Tischbein, 'Jeune Fille jouant de la mandoline' (1772).

being suitable for either violin or mandoline, and often also for par-dessus de viole or flute.

The mandoline's rise in popularity at this time made it a frequent accoutrement in portraits of the period. A fine example is Pierre Lacour le Père's portrait of André-François-Benoit-Elisabeth Leberthon, vicomte de Virelade (Illustration 5*a*), which gives a clear view of the seated playing position. However, the mandoline's visual attractiveness became of particular importance to fashion-conscious women. François-Hubert Drouais's portrait of Madame de Pompadour, completed in 1764 and now in the National Gallery, London, is one of the first appearances of the mandoline in French art. Over the next few years it was frequently included in female portraits, such as Johann Heinrich Tischbein's 'Jeune fille jouant de la mandoline' of 1772[6] (Illustration 5*b*), where the mandoline functions partly as an instrument and partly as an ornament. This association between the mandoline

[6] Sold at Sotheby's, New York, 19 Dec. 1973.

and women is highlighted by the title of the first tutor to be published for the instrument, Gervasio's *Méthode très facile Pour apprendre à jouer de la Mandoline à quatre Cordes Instrument fait pour les Dames* (Paris, 1767).

Giovanni Battista Gervasio was a touring virtuoso/composer, active in the 1760s, but whose only appearance at a *concert spirituel* was not until 24 December 1784, when he played a mandoline concerto of his own composition.[7] Although he published several works in Paris and London, the bulk of his very large output remains in manuscript collections, particularly F:Pn and S:Uu.

Table 1, compiled from various Parisian journals and almanachs, and from information given on the title-pages of published music from the period, shows the years in which the various *maîtres de mandoline* in Paris are known to have been giving lessons on the instrument. As information is not available for every year, the table includes only years when these musicians were advertising their services.

TABLE 1: Maîtres de Mandoline in Paris

Barrois	1789	
Pietro Denis	1765–77	(1775 in England)
Fouquet/Fouchetti	1770–89	(previously in Lyon)
Frizieri/Frixeri	1775–6	(blind)
Martin	1777–9	
Mazzuchelli	1777–87	
Merchi	1766–89	(resident in Paris previously as a performer and teacher of the colascione and guitar)
Riggieri	*c.*1781–83	(see the comment on the Riggieri entries under 'Instrumental Music Published in Paris 1781–3' in Appendix III)
Sody	1759–89	(resident in Paris as a mandolinist since 1749. He is noted as blind after 1775)
(le) Vasseur	1778–83	
Veginy	*c.*1768	
Verdone	1788–9	(previously in Lyon)
Vernier	1778–83	

---

[7] *Mercure de France*, Jan. 1785, 81. NB At this time the term 'concerto' did not necessarily signify a work with full orchestra. Often it was used simply in the sense of a combined performance, i.e. with at least one other player. Most eighteenth-century compositions designated as mandolin concertos are in any case intended to be performed with only two violins and basso continuo as accompaniment to the soloist.

Two of these *maîtres*, not yet mentioned, are of particular importance: Pietro Denis and Giovanni Fouchetti. Denis[8] features prominently in Parisian records, not only as a *maître* but also as a prolific composer and arranger for the mandoline. His most important work was his three-volume *Méthode* (Paris, 1768, 1769, and 1773) in which he teaches violinists how to transfer their technique to the mandoline, and how to provide accompaniments to the latest songs from the Comédie Italienne.

In volume I, Denis explains his reasons for publishing the tutor. The public, he says, have asked him to produce a work which will enable violinists, without the aid or expense of a *maître*, to master the mandoline. This is not a complex matter, according to Denis:

> It is in no way necessary to detail here all the ancient customs, good and bad, and to deliver a long verbiage of rules which certain people falsely imagine to be of some use . . . I have seen, in Naples, Mr Julien, whom I believe to be the finest mandolinist, and who assured me that no one has fixed or decided the strokes of the plectrum. (Denis 1768, 3.)

In spite of this, Denis mentions later that the eye of a good *maître* is worth more than any amount of written instruction. And, lest there be any doubt as to which teacher he has in mind, he continues: 'Besides, I can, in six lessons, position the hand and accomplish everything that I have proposed, for the price of thirty-six *livres* payable in advance'. (Denis 1768, 10.)

This first volume of the *Méthode* appeared in April 1768 (*Annonces, affiches et avis divers*, 25 April 1768, p. 368), and whether or not Denis had any of his colleagues in mind when he wrote dismissively of 'a long verbiage of rules', it is clear that Leoné was stung into reply when his own tutor appeared in May of the same year (*Annonces, affiches et avis divers*, 26 May 1768, p. 464).

---

[8] Biographical dictionaries (e.g. Choron/Fayole (1810) and Fétis (1873)) list Denis as a Frenchman born in Provence, and credit him with the authorship of a *méthode de chant* (*c*.1750) in addition to numerous works for the mandoline. However, in the *Annonces, affiches et avis divers* (Paris) for 11 March 1765 the death is noted of 'Sr. Denis, musicien'. I believe this to be the author of the *méthode de chant*. The first work to appear for mandoline by Pietro Denis, a set of six duets, was not published until 1764, fourteen years after the *méthode de chant*. Indeed it is possible that the mandolinist was not French but Italian. His Christian name is of course Italian, and in the *Annonces* for 11 June 1767 he is named as Sr. Denisi (p. 483). While it is common to find Italians frenchifying their names in Paris at this time, the reverse is rare, so Denisi may have become Denis, just as Leoni became Leoné.

In the preface to this work, Leoné states that many people have requested a set of rules from him for playing the mandoline, and that his *Méthode* was written in response to this request:

I determined to do this, partly owing to the lack of teachers capable of demonstrating the instrument adequately in a region where it is not well known, but still more because I believed that I had to remedy a defective treatise which has already appeared on this subject. (Leoné 1768, 1.)

This remark is presumably directed at Denis, and towards the end of the text Leoné has squeezed in the following remarks in small type at the bottom of a page, suggesting that he could not contain his annoyance that Denis had managed to publish first!

It is a mistake to think that the mandoline is an easy instrument. Those who undertake to teach it in twelve lessons must have got their principles, and in consequence their music, from some famous Neapolitan stroller. But it is much easier to discover in them the true portrait of a Quack, and the love of money, than it is even to learn how to tune the instrument in so short a time. (Ibid. 19.)

Giovanni Fouchetti (the French form of his name, Jean Fouquet, was also used) came to Paris in late 1769 from Lyon. His *Méthode* was published in Paris by Sieber during summer or autumn of 1771,[9] and was the only one of the Paris tutors to be written both for mandoline and mandolino. Although this was the only work for mandolin which Sieber ever published, it was still included in his catalogue in 1800 and indeed was listed in the *Handbuch der Musikalischen Litteratur* of Carl Friedrich Whistling and Friedrich Hofmeister (Leipzig, 1817–27), which listed published music available in Vienna and Leipzig. This longevity is probably due to the fact that the mandolino enjoyed a renewed popularity in the years around 1800 in Vienna, temporarily eclipsing the Neapolitan mandoline.

In the tutor, Fouchetti makes it clear that he prefers the mandolino:

This instrument is not as difficult to play as the four-course mandoline, because one doesn't have to move up the neck as often. Also it is preferred to the other type at present, and is considered more harmonious, though this is a question of taste. (Fouchetti 1771, 5.)

[9] This date has been deduced from Sieber's catalogues, reproduced and dated by Johansson (1955).

However, despite Fouchetti's assertion that the mandolino was preferred, the mandoline was the dominant instrument in Paris at the time, and even the 'Six Serinates' and 'Six Sonates' found at the end of his *Méthode* are written with the four-course instrument in mind.

Besides Gervasio, Denis, Leoné, and Fouchetti, one other musician published a *méthode de mandoline* in Paris. This was Michel Corrette, whose *Nouvelle Méthode* was published in Paris, Lyon and Dunkirk in September 1772 (*Annonces, affiches et avis divers*, 14 September 1772, 779). Corrette, as well as pursuing a career as organist and composer, produced more than a dozen tutor books for a variety of instruments including violin, cello, guitar, musette, and flute. There is no evidence of any special association between Corrette and the mandoline and many parts of his tutor bear a marked resemblance to the earlier Parisian *Méthodes*. However, as Corrette was by far the most educated musician to produce a tutor for the mandoline, this is a particularly valuable work.

During the period 1761–83, approximately eighty-five volumes of music for mandoline were published in Paris, consisting mostly of duets for two mandolines, sonatas for mandoline and bass, and songs with mandoline accompaniment. (See Appendix III for a complete list.) Although the majority of the works are by composers closely connected with the mandoline, it is noteworthy that, in the years around 1770, several violinists/composers (or their publishers) designated their music as being suitable for either violin or mandoline. A typical case is that of the *Six Sonates*, Op. 3 by Valentin Roeser. When these were first published in 1769 (*Annonces, affiches et avis divers*, 3 April 1769), they were intended for two violins and bass, but the title-page stated that they 'could be performed on the mandoline'. However, later editions of the same work made no mention of mandoline at all. As they were originally dedicated to the Duc de Chartres (who employed Leoné as *maître de mandoline*) the mention of the mandoline may have been simply a diplomatic gesture to Roeser's aristocratic patron.

The most common instrumental combination was the mandoline duet. As Coates remarks, (1977, 77) mandolines were often made in matching pairs in the eighteenth century, and their portable nature made them ideal for alfresco playing, the second instrument giving a harmonic fullness not readily obtainable on a single mandoline. The duets were usually in the form of two-movement sonatas, or a collection of minuets, allemandes, or other dance forms. The sonatas for mandoline and bass are most commonly full three-movement sonatas, and are generally of a much greater technical difficulty than the duets. Many of the compositions of this period are perfect examples of the *style galant*, just as the mandoline itself perfectly encapsulated the eighteenth-century love of simplicity and elegance.

Despite the great popularity of the mandoline at this time, there are few occasions other than those mentioned above on which the instrument was heard at the *Concert Spirituel*. Although the mandoline had been developed with public performance in mind, it was still quiet when compared to the standard orchestral instruments. This lack of volume was remarked upon by the reviewer from the *Journal de Musique* (November 1770, 43) after a performance by Mlle. de Villeneuve, the only woman mandolinist ever to play at a *concert spirituel*:

Mademoiselle de VILLENEUVE . . . performed a mandoline concerto, composed by M. Frizeri, with all the art, and with all the great execution of the most skilful master. She gave greater pleasure than one could have expected from an instrument which is too dry, and too lacking in resonance, to be heard in a large hall.

Apart from her, only two other mandolinists appeared there: M. Aldaye (Alday), aged seven or eight, who in March 1771 'played the mandoline with a facility and a rapidity of execution which was most extraordinary';[10] and M. Nonnini, who performed on two occasions, 8 and 24 December 1783, when he played a mandoline concerto of his own composition, and received a warm reception: 'This instrument, regarded as unsuitable for a large concert hall, achieved, under his fingers, a mellowness and a perfection which one would have believed impossible; he was applauded enthusiastically.' (*Journal de Paris*, quoted from Le Roux 1986.) Nonnini stayed in Paris for some time and gave several self-promoted concerts in addition to his appearances at the *Concert Spirituel*. However, the *halle des Cents Suisses*, where the *Concert Spiritual* was held, was too large a venue to succeed with plucked-instrument performances on more than an occasional basis. Small-scale private concerts were not reviewed by Parisian journals of this period, and therefore it may be inferred that the bulk of peformances by mandolinists have gone unrecorded.

In Lyon the mandoline achieved popularity earlier than in Paris, presumably due to its closer proximity to Naples, and to the presence there of many

---

[10] *Journal de Musique* Mar. 1771, 218. Alday later became a successful violinist.

Italians. Giovanni Fouchetti was teaching mandoline there from 1757[11] and the *Affiches de Lyon* for 16 May 1759 announced two further teachers:

For a little while in this town there have been two Venetians who teach an instrument called the mandoline; they already have many male and female students, and those who wish to augment their number should address themselves to the Swiss House, rue Raisin, near the Place des Jacobins, where they are living. They ought to remain for a while in our town.

It is clear from advertisements of the period that both types of mandolin coexisted in Lyon.[12] However, the considerable quantity of music written by Lyonnais mandolinists during the 1760s and 1770s which has survived, especially the works of Verdone (MSS in F:Pn) and Fouchetti, is clearly for mandoline.

Table 2 has been compiled from the pages of the *Affiches de Lyon*, giving dates when the various *maîtres de mandoline* are known to have been teaching in Lyon. As was the case with the Parisian *maîtres*, information is not available for every year and the dates given are those on which the musicians are known to have advertised their services.

TABLE 2: Maîtres de Mandoline in Lyon

Biferi the younger	1767–70	(A Neapolitan)
Cremasqui/ Cremaschy	1764–68	(This Italian musician specialised in mandolino, which he also sold, and taught the art of vocal accompaniment on the mandolin)[13]
'Deux Venetiens'	1759	
Dubrec fils	1771	(A pupil of Leoné, Dubrec charged 9 *livres* a month for lessons at his house, or 15 *livres* in town)[14]
Fouquet/Fouchetti, Giovanni	1757–69	(He then moved to Paris)

[11] The 1761 *Almanach de Lyon* gives this date for Fouchetti's first listing. Vallas (1932) quotes many of the following extracts from the *Affiches de Lyon*. However, his listing of Vicinelli as having taught since 1756 (p. 341) is mistaken; the correct date is 1763.

[12] See for example *Affiches de Lyon* 30 Sept. 1761: 'Two mandolines, made in Italy. One has six strings, the other four'.

[13] *Affiches de Lyon* 21 Nov. 1764: 'Sr. Cremaschy, an Italian, continues to teach the 12-string mandolin in this town.'

[14] *Affiches de Lyon* 3 Jan. 1771: 'Pupil of Sr. Leoni ... His principles are the same as those of Sr. Leoni, and he prides himself on deserving the attention of the public through the rapid progress made by those who come to him.'

Gatti, Pierre	1760–5	
Grou	1761–5	(Also a luthier, making mandolines): see *Affiches de Lyon*, 2 Mar. 1763)
Joannot	1764–70	(Died 1770, aged 32. Also taught violin, cello, singing, par-dessus de viole: see Vallas 1932, 341)
Juspin	1764	(also violin)
Tauseany	1765–6	(also taught lute, guitar, par-dessus de viole)[15]
Verdone	1768	(He later moved to Paris)[16]
Vicinelli, the brothers	1763–5	(Romans)

Fouchetti, a student of Leoné, is known to have sold his music in manuscript at this time, and also to have sold Italian mandolines.[17] As was the case in Paris, Italian instruments were more highly prized than those made in France. Italian instruments were frequently offered for sale, for example one by Joseph Walner Taurini of Naples in 1759 (*Affiches de Lyon*, 23 May 1759). Amongst the Lyonnais luthiers making mandolines were Mériotte, Pierre Kettenhoven, Picchi, and Serriere (*Affiches de Lyon*, 4 April 1764, 26 March 1772, 3 February 1763, and 5 October 1768 respectively). The chief music retailers were the brothers le Goux, who were selling music by Leoné in 1761 (*Affiches de Lyon*, 16 December 1761), and Castaud who announced that so many copies of Leoné's new *Méthode* had been sold in 1769, the year after its publication in Paris, that he had run out of supplies (*Affiches de Lyon*, 25 January 1769). The mandolino was featured in a concert at the Académie in Lyon on 2 March 1768 when Cremasqui, newly returned from Italy, performed a sonata there (*Affiches de Lyon*, 2 March 1768). Vallas (1908, 10) notes that mandolins were included in the Académie des Beaux-Arts' orchestra in the years around 1760 in order to reinforce the upper parts. However, the Académie modelled its concerts on the *Concert Spirituel* in Paris and was therefore geared more to orchestral works than to chamber music, so little more is known about mandoline performers in Lyon.

[15] Several pieces for lute by *Tauseana* survive in a MS in Köln-Universitäts und Stadbibliothek Ms.1.N.68. The *Affiches de Lyon* for 2 Sept. 1772 mentions a performance of an air by 'sieur Tozeani'.

[16] *Affiches de Lyon* 14 Apr. 1768: 'Sieur. Verdone, an Italian musician, proposes to stay in this town for some time, offering his services to persons who wish to learn to play the mandoline; he asks for only 3 months to make good students, as he has already done in London and in Paris, with his own method of simplifying all the principles.'

[17] *Affiches de Lyon* 13 Aug. 1760: 'Sr. Fouquet, pupil of the best Paris *maîtres* of the par-dessus de viole, offers to teach how to play the mandoline, which he learnt himself from Sr. Leoni.'

Elsewhere in France the mandoline made a more modest appearance, but was a popular amateur instrument. Tobias Smollett, while in Nice on 6 December 1763, made the following observation:

We have likewise made acquaintance with some other individuals, particularly with Mr. St. Pierre, junior, who is a considerable merchant, and consul for Naples. He is a well-bred, sensible young man, speaks English, is an excellent performer on the lute and mandolin, and has a pretty collection of books. In a word, I hope we shall pass the winter agreeably enough. (Tobias Smollett 1766, 1: 215, letter 12.)

This highlights the fact that the influence of the Neapolitan instrument was spread not only through the skill of a few professional players, but also through contact with visitors to Naples.

A search through provincial journals of this period reveals countless advertisements for luthiers making mandolines, and for retailers importing and selling Italian instruments and strings.[18] But by the 1780s the worsening economic and political situation in France put an end to the escapist pursuits of the aristocratic elites. Apart from the appearances of Gervasio and Nonnini at the *Concert Spirituel* (already noted), the mandoline made little further impression on musical life, either in Paris or elsewhere in France.

[18] A typical example is J. Charles, a luthier, formerly of Paris, who settled in Marseilles and, amongst a wide range of instruments from violins to harps to serinettes, made mandolines (Gourand 1908, 179). There seem to be no examples of French luthiers specializing in mandolines however, in the way that Neapolitan families such as the Vinaccias did.

8

The Mandoline elsewhere in Europe

Great Britain

The mandolino was introduced into Britain early in the eighteenth century when Fr. Conti (see Chapter 3) performed at Mr Hickford's dancing room in James Street, London, on 2 April 1707: 'The Signior Conti will play upon his great Theorbo, and on the Mandoline, an instrument not known yet'.[1] This instrument enjoyed aristocratic patronage in subsequent decades, as Philip Mercier's portrait of the Royal Family testifies. In this painting (National Gallery, London; reproduced in Tyler 1981*a*), Princess Caroline is depicted playing the mandolino.

However the mandolin never attained the popularity in Britain that it enjoyed in many other parts of Europe. Indeed the terms *mandolin*, *mandola*, and *mandolino* appear to have been used to cover a number of instruments, as this excerpt from a letter by Dr Clephane of the Rose of Kilravock family indicates:

10 March 1758 . . . The spinet, too, has its merit, and has more than the instrument I once proposed for you—the guitarre, or the mandolino, as it is called here by our London ladies. What induced me to recommend it is its portableness, and that methinks music is well as an amusement, but not as a study. However, if you have once made some progress on the spinet or harpsichord, the mandola will be an easy acquisition. (The Spalding Club 1848, 461.)

This compounding of the terms *guitar* and *mandolin* is also met with in the first published music for the instrument: 'Eighteen D I V E R T I-M E N T O S for two Guitars or two Mandelins. Properly adapted by the best Masters. Printed for J. Oswald on the Pavement St. Martin's Churchyard, London (1757)'. The music contained in this volume is quite unlike any mandolin music to be found in Paris or Vienna, consisting entirely of melodic lines with no double-stopping, and with a lower limit of d'. It is

---

[1] John Aston (1882, ii: 38). This is the first use of the word 'mandolin' recorded in the Oxford English Dictionary.

probable that the instrument referred to in Britain at this time as the mandolin was a type of cittern known as the 'English Guittar', which had only recently been introduced into the country.[2]

However, by the late 1760s the term seems to have been regularly used to describe the Neapolitan instrument. G. B. Gervasio helped to popularize the mandoline when, on 3 March 1768, he played a mandoline concerto during one of the intervals of Barthélemon's opera *Oithona*, at the Haymarket Theatre, London (Fiske 1973, 261; Highfill 1978; Gervasio was referred to as 'Signor Gervasia'). He also published a volume entitled 'Airs for the mandoline, guittar, violon or german flute, interspersed with songs . . .' at about the same time.[3] The mandoline was also featured at a concert in the Holywell Music Room in Oxford in December 1771: 'Three *Italian musicians* are engaged on Monday next to perform some select Pieces on the Calisoncino, the Roman Guittar, and Maundolins'.[4]

The only tutor for the mandoline published at this time in Britain was an English translation of Leoné's *Méthode*, published by Longman and Broderip (London, 1785),[5] although a tutor for the Genoese mandolin attributed to Francesco Conti also survives in manuscript.[6] However, British lack of familiarity with the instrument, and continued confusion over its name, is illustrated in this passage from Samuel Pegge's *Anonymania*, written in 1796:

When the instrument now coming into use is called a Mandarin, we are led to think it to be something used by the Chinese Lords or Mandarins; but the truer pronunciation is *Mandolin*, for I suppose it has no connexion with the chinese nation, but rather is an Italian instrument, or *citara*; and the correct way of writing and pronouncing is *mandola*, which, in Altieri's Dictionary is explained by a *citern*. *Mandola* signifies in

[2] Described more fully by Robert Spencer and Ian Harwood in 'English Guitar'. *New Grove Dictionary of Musical Instruments* (1984). A more recent article can be found in *Early Music* 15 (1987), 205–18 by Philip Coggin: ' "This Easy and Agreable Instrument", A History of the English Guittar'.

[3] The sole surviving copy, in GB:Lbl, is at present missing.

[4] Jackson's *Oxford Journal* 14 Dec. 1771. John H. Mee (1911) gives a full account of the Oxford Music Room concerts, from 1748 onwards. Parisian journals record Pietro Denis as being in England during 1775 and *Grove* (1954, 5: 548) states that Leoné performed on the mandoline at Hickford's Rooms, London, on 17 March 1766.

[5] 'A complete introduction to the art of playing the mandoline, containing the most essential rules and examples for learners to obtain a proficiency . . .'.

[6] 'l'accordo della Mandola è l'istesso della Chitarra alla francese SCOLA del Leutino, osìa Mandolino alla Genovese.' (*c*.1770–80; MS in GB:Ge.) See Ch. 10 for details of the Genoese mandolin. This is not the Conti mentioned earlier, but may be his son.

Italian an *Almond*; which shews that it takes its name from the figure of its belly, which is much like an almond. (S. Pegge 1796 [1809], 49.)

Prague, Vienna, and Germany

During the period 1760–85, when the mandoline enjoyed great popularity in Paris, the Habsburg Empire accorded it a more modest place in music-making. Charles Burney, in his *Musical Tour* of 1771, noted its appearance at M. l'Augier's concert in Vienna, in this extract dated 3 September 1770:

The room was much too crowded for full pieces: some trios only were played by Signor Giorgi, a scholar of Tartini, Conforte, a scholar of Pugnani, and by Count Brühl, who is an excellent performer on many instruments, particularly the violin, violoncello and mandoline. The pieces they executed were composed by Huber, a poor man, who plays the tenor at the playhouse; but it was excellent music, simple, clear, rich in good harmony, and frequently abounding with fancy and contrivance. (Burney 1771, 2: 97.)

G. B. Gervasio is recorded as having played in Frankfurt-am-Main on 10 December 1777 (Wölki 1984, 10). However it was not until the late 1780s, at precisely the time when the mandoline's fortunes were waning in France, that the instrument attained a higher status in Central Europe.

Prague was at this time second only to Vienna as an artistic centre within the Habsburg Empire and, although the mandoline never achieved there the popularity it had enjoyed in Paris, the instrument did attain some success in this city, and acquired several important repertoire items there. Prague luthiers, such as Charles Joseph Hellmer and Joseph Antoine Laske, made copies of Italian mandolines, but more importantly both Mozart and Beethoven composed there for the instrument.

Mozart, having already composed *Don Giovanni* in Vienna during the summer of 1787, added the mandolin aria 'Deh, vieni alla finestra' while rehearsing the singers for the first performance.[7] This appearance of a serenading mandolinist, although probably inspired by the success of similar

[7] Mann (1977) gives further details. The singer was Luigi Bassi and the mandolinist Jean-Baptiste Kucharz (who also made the piano arrangements of many of Mozart's operas). Two other Mozart songs with mandolin accompaniment, 'Die Zufriedenheit' and 'An die Zither' are in the catalogue of D-ddr:Bds Mus. 15210. The original MSS have been missing since World War II. A modern edition can be found in *Wolfgang Amadeus Mozart. Neue Ausgabe sämtlicher Werke. Serie III, werkgruppe 8. Lieder* (Basel, 1963).

rtrayals in Grétry's *L'Amant jaloux* (Paris, 1778) and Paisiello's *Barber of* *eville* (St Petersburg, 1782, revised Paris, 1784), certainly crystallized the ole of the instrument in 'serious' music for succeeding generations of composers, who have used it mainly as an instrument for serenades. Of Beethoven's four compositions for the mandoline, it is probable that at least three were written in Prague. In 1796, at the request of Prince Lichnowsky, Beethoven visited the city, where he met the Count Clam Gallas and the Countess-to-be, Josephine Clary, a mandoline pupil of Kucharz. For her he composed the Sonatina in C (WoO 44a), Variations in D (WoO 44b), and the Adagio in E♭ (WoO 43b). A fourth piece, Sonatina in C minor (WoO 43a)[8] was probably composed for a Viennese friend, Wenzel Krumpholz, a violinist and mandolinist.

The Národní Muzeum in Prague has a large collection of manuscript mandoline music from this period, including a considerable amount of chamber music.[9] The composers represented include Padre Bernardo Arauhal, (including six quartets for mandoline, violin, viola, and cello), Jan Ladislav Dussik (two quartets for mandoline, violin, viola and mandolono) and Megelin (a divertimento for mandoline, violin, and mandolono) and the collection includes the earliest known parts for the bass mandolone (see Ch. 10).

The mandolin achieved a higher public profile in the last years of the eighteenth century, due to the appearance of the virtuoso performer and composer, Bartholomeo Bortolazzi, a Brescian.[10] Johann Nepomuk Hummel composed his Mandolin Concerto of 1799 (GB: Lbl. Add. 32216) expressly for this performer, who toured principally in Germany and around Vienna. Serious music critics, such as those of the *Allgemeine musikalische Zeitung* (published in Leipzig by Breitkopf & Härtel) were not easily convinced of the value of a small plucked instrument: '*Dresden* 2 September 1803 . . . About Bortolazzi, the mandolin player, I say nothing except that he

---

[8] The manuscript of the Sonatina in C minor can be found in GB:Lbl. add. 29801, ff. 87. The other manuscripts are to be found, as follows: Sonatina in C—CS-ČSSR Friedland; Variations in D—CS-ČSSR Reichenberg; Adagio in E♭—CS-ČSSR Reichenberg (These collections now form part of CS-ČSSR:Pnm.) A modern edition of all four pieces ed. V. Hladky is available (Wilhelmshaven, Heinrichshofen's Verlag).

[9] I am indebted to Stephen Morey for drawing my attention to this collection.

[10] Fétis (1873) states that Bortolazzi was born in Venice in 1773, but Wölki (1984) suggests that he was born in Toscolano, Lake Garda, in Brescia. Bortolazzi published a tutor: *Anweisung die Mandoline von selbst zu erlernen* (Leipzig, 1805).

does a lot. But what a poor tool that only chirps and cannot hold a note in order to produce a singing melody'. (*AMZ* September 1803, 836). But Bortolazzi's skill won over many to his side, as this review from the same periodical grudgingly admits:

Herr Bortolazzi. Virtuoso on the mandolin. On the mandolin? many readers repeated, shaking their heads and grinning. So be it. Though it is true that this small, limited, chirpy instrument, which is well-played by few, has gained little credit in Germany, Hr. B. gives a sterling demonstration, with imagination and feeling. Tastefully and with unflagging industry he is able to speak through this paltry instrument [*unbedeutendes Organ*]. His concertos with full orchestra are, by their very nature, of little interest: but his Variations and similar small pieces (mostly with his seven-year-old son, who accompanies well on the guitar), and also his improvisations, are most delightful and well worth hearing. Scarcely anyone at all, other than an Italian, would be inclined to become skilled in such a small interest. Hr. B. has also published pleasing compositions for his instrument; others are still to appear. (19 October 1803, 45–6.)

Bortolazzi specialized in performances on the Cremonese or Brescian mandolin, an instrument tuned in the same way as the Neapolitan mandoline, but with single strings and a softer tone (see Chapters 9 and 10). In Vienna, in the early nineteenth century, the Neapolitan mandoline, Cremonese mandolin, and mandolino all took their part in music-making, all three being referred to simply as 'mandolin'. The *Handbuch der Musikalischen Litteratur* by Carl Friedrich Whistling and Friedrich Hofmeister (1817), a catalogue published for the music trade, lists the following works:

Composer	Title	Library Copy	Date
Aichelbourg (d)	*Potpourri*, Op. 1 (mand. or vn. and gtr.)	——	1812
	Variations, Op. 2 (mand. or vn. and gtr.)	——	1812
	Notturno conc., Op. 3 (mand. or vn. and gtr.)	——	1812
	Variations conc., Op. 4 (mand. or vn. and gtr.)	A:Wn	1812
Bortolazzi (B)	*Six Variations* (*Nel cor più*), Op. 8 (mand. or vn. and gtr.)	CS-ČSSR: Pnm	1804
	Sonate, Op. 9 (mand. or vn. and pf.)	A:Wgm	1804
	6 Thèmes variés, Op. 16 (mand. or vn. and gtr.)	A:Wgm, D-brd:B	1803
	Anweisung die Mandoline von selbst zu erlernen	F:Pn, B:Br	1805

(*continued overleaf*)

Composer	Title	Library Copy	Date
Call (L. de)	*Variations*, Op. 8 (mand. or vn. and gtr.)	A:Wn	1803
	Sonate conc., Op. 108 (mand. or vn. and gtr.)	A:Wn	1811
	Variations, Op. 111 (mand. or vn. and gtr.)	GB:Lbl	1812
Fouchetti (G)	*Méthode de Mandoline à 4 et à 6 cordes*	F:Pn	1771
Zucconi (T. de)	*6 Variations* (mand. or vn. and gtr.)	——	*c.*1810

(The publication dates given are my own additions, compiled from notices in the *Allgemeine musikalische Zeitung* and, in some cases, from unpublished research conducted by Marga Wilden-Hüsgen of Aachen.)

Other works published in Vienna in the early years of the nineteenth century include:

Composer	Title	Library Copy	Date
Bortolazzi (B)	*Variations*, Op. 10	D-brd:B	*c.*1804
	6 variations sur une piece d'Alcine (mand. and gtr.)	——	1802
Call (L. de)	*Variations pour la Mandoline ou le Violon et la Guitarre sur la lire qui dove ride l'aura*, Op. 25	A:Wn	1804–5
Hoffmann, (J)	*Tre Duetti*, Op. 1 (2 mands.)	GB:Lbl	1799
	Tre Duetti, Op. 2 (2 mands.)	——	1799
Hummel (J. N.)	*Grande Sonata per il Clavicembalo o Pianoforte con accompagnemento di mandolino o violino obligato.*	A:Wgm	1810
Neuhauser	*Notturno per il mandolino*	——	*c.*1799
Neuling, V.	*Sonata für Pianoforte und Violine oder Mandoline*, Op. 3.	I:Mc	1813

The Viennese music-dealer Johann Traeg issued a list in 1799 of manuscript music available from his shop in the Singerstrasse, which included:

1 Anonymo   *Serenata per il Mandolino e Viola*
2 Anonymo   *Sonate p. detto Violino e B in B*
3 Anonymo   *Sonata p. 2 Mandolini in G*
4 Anonymo   *Sonata p. 2 detto in B*
5 Hoffmann (Giov) *Trio p. il Mand. e B*
6 Anonymo   *Serenata p. il Mand. e Viola in C*

7	Anonymo	*detto detto in F*
8	Anonymo	*detto detto in D*
9	Anonymo	*Cassazione p. il Mand. V. Viola e Vllo*
10	Anonymo	*Quartetto p. detto detto in D*
11	Anonymo	*detto detto in A*
12	Schlik	*Son. p. il Mandolino e Basso*
13	Anonymo	*Quartetto p. il Mand. V. Viola e B*
14	Anonymo	*Aria p. il Mandolino*
15	Anonymo	*Trio à Mand. Viola e B*
16	Neuhauser	*Noturno p. il Mandolino &c*

taken from Zuth, 1931, 94).

Giovanni (or Johann) Hoffmann also issued a number of works in manu-script, through Traeg in 1799, including *III Quartetti per il Mandolino, Viola, V. et Vc.* and *III Serenate à Mandolino e Viola*.

While it is not possible here to outline the development of the mandoline in every country, two more important areas should be mentioned. The first appearance of the mandoline in America was in 1769 when John (Giovanni) Gualdo, an Italian wine merchant and music-dealer in Philadelphia, played 'a solo upon the Mandolino' (Hambly 1977, 5). Assuming this to be the same Giovanni Gualdo who published 'Six Easy Evening Entertainments for Two Mandolins or Two Violins with a Thorough Bass for the Harpsichord or Violoncello . . .' in London, then it may be assumed that his performance was given on the Neapolitan instrument. Gualdo died in a fall from his house in 1771.

On 17 June 1774, in the same city, a concert was given 'for the benefit of Signor Sodi, first dancing master of the Opera in Paris and London, in which Mr Vidal who has been a musician of the Chambers of the King of Portugal will play on diverse instruments of music'. During the concert, Vidal played 'a duetto on the mandolino, accompanied with the violin'. (Gladd 1987, 7.)

In Russia, the Genoese mandolinist Zaneboni enjoyed a great success during the early 1780s. This performer, who lived in Liege from about 1770,[11] made numerous tours throughout Europe performing his own com-positions:

---

[11] Mooser (1948–51, 2) gives fuller information on Zaneboni and other performers in Moscow and St Petersburg.

5 January 1782, Moscow . . . Monsieur Zaneboni has the honour to announce that, next Friday 7th January, in the *salla des masquerades* of Mr Maddox, after the comedy, he will give, on the mandolin, a vocal and instrumental concert, in the course of which he will perform many pieces of his own composition, namely:

1) A symphony for full orchestra
2) A concerto for mandolin
3) Mlle. Vigna will sing an italian air
4) A symphony
5) A solo with variations, for the mandolin
6) An italian air
7) A rondo for the mandolin
8) A symphony . . . (*Gazette de Moscou*, 5 January 1782, quoted in Mooser 1948–51, 2: 322.)

Zaneboni (incorrectly called *Sannebuoni* by Gerber, 1790) appeared again in Moscow, on 25 February 1782, 'sur la véritable mandoline' (*Gazette de Moscou*, 23 February 1782). In St Petersburg he performed on 15 April 1781 at the *Théâtre du Pont-Rouge* during a performance of Beaumarchais' *Barber of Seville* (*Gazette de S. Petersbourg*, 13 April 1781). This may well have persuaded Paisiello, who was at that time in the service of the Russian Court, to use the mandoline in his operatic setting of the work, which received its first performance in St Petersburg in the following year.

Another mandolinist (and singer) was L. Invernardi, who toured Russia *c.*1795 with the violinist and singer Francesco Giordani. The duo performed throughout Europe, including Danzig, Stockholm, and Königsberg. Invernardi also performed in Hamburg in 1799 (Mooser, vol. 2, 662 and 631).

9

A Guide to Playing the Neapolitan Mandoline*

The Instrument

Several of the Paris tutors give illustrations of the mandoline; Leoné, Denis, and Corrette (see Illustrations 6–9). The Corrette example is quite unlike any known instrument of the period and seems to be simply the result of poor drawing; however the other three drawings offer us a great deal of information.

Late eighteenth- and early nineteenth-century orchestration tutors usually give the range of the mandoline as being g–d''' (Albrechtsberger 1790; Kastner 1837). However Denis's instrument has fourteen frets giving a top note of f#''', while Leoné's has sixteen frets and an upper limit of g#'''. The discrepancy is explained by extra frets beyond the tenth (where the neck joins the body) inlaid into the table of the instrument. These extra frets are usually made from ebony or ivory unlike the lower frets which, as Gervasio mentions, are of brass (Gervasio 1767, 2). The first movement of the Second Sonata from Leoné's Op. II (published by Bailleux) requires still one more fret in order to play several top a''' semiquavers (Ex. 1). Fouchetti confirms this use of extra frets as being

Ex. 1

Leoné Op. II, sonata 2, 1st. mvt.

* This chapter is based on the Parisian tutors of Gervasio, Denis, Leoné, Fouchetti, and Corrette, and the Leipzig tutor of Bortolazzi.

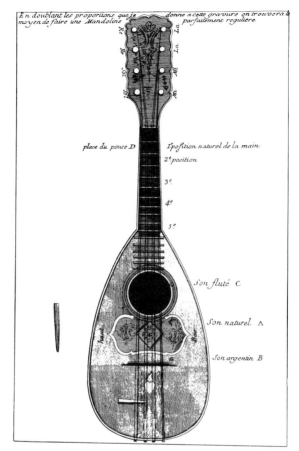

Illustration 6. Mandoline, from Leoné, *Méthode* (1768).

common on the four-course mandoline: 'There are ten frets on the fingerboard of the mandoline, and several others on the table of the instrument, which are used when one has to change position.' (Fouchetti 1771, 3.) These extra frets are rarely encountered on the mandolino, because the tenth fret on the g'' course gives f''', a sufficiently high top note for most plucked string music of the period.

Neapolitan mandolines have always carried a protective scratch-plate with a distinctive batwing shape, unlike that of the Genoese which is traditionally shaped like a parallelogram. Modern instruments carry a tortoise-shell plate but, as Corrette relates, on many early instruments:

there is a plaque of hard wood, such as ebony, grénadille, palissande etc. and which

Illustration 7. Mandoline, from Denis, *Méthode*, I (1768).

Illustration 8. Mandoline, from Denis, *Méthode*, III (1773).

Illustration 9. Mandoline, from Corrette, *Nouvelle méthode* (1772).

instrument-makers have put there so that quill strokes do not scratch the table, because beginners are subject to this fault. (Corrette 1772, 1.)

Fouchetti mentions that both the four- and six-course instruments are termed mandolins. However, according to Leoné:

there are some other instruments of a roughly similar form which one calls *Mandoles* in Italy, and which foreigners often confuse with the one under discussion here, which is the most perfect and which ought justly to participate in the prerogatives of the Violin, recognised as the most universal and widely used instrument. (Leoné 1768, 1.)

Instruments were built in France as well as imported from Naples. However, there is no doubt that the latter were the more highly prized, as can be seen from an examination of inventories of luthiers' effects:

Inventaire après le décès du Sieur François Lejeune. 21 Sept. 1785 . . . Item deux mandolines de Naples et quatre communes . . . (Paris, Archive National: Min. Centr. CXXII, 850)

Inventaire après le décès de Marie-Jeune Dupuis femme Lejeune. 29 Sept. 1801 . . . Item trois mandolines de Naples à quatre cordes prisé à raison de quatre francs chaque revenant à douze francs cy. . . . 12 fr. Item huit mandolines communes prisé quatre francs ci. . . . 4 fr. (Paris, Archive National: Min. Centr. LXXIII, 1168) (taken from Milliot 1970, 222–31).

This distinction between a highly-priced Neapolitan instrument and a cheaper 'commune' mandoline can be found in all musical inventories of the period.

Stringing

It is a common assumption that the canted table of the mandoline was introduced to counteract the greater tension of metal strings. Yet the Paris tutors reveal that all metal stringing was not customary at this time: 'As regards the e″, use gut strings, taking the *chanterelles* of the *Par-dessus de viole*.' (Fouchetti 1771, 5.) Corrette confirms this use of gut: 'As regards the quality of the strings, use the *chanterelles* of the guitar for the [e″] strings.' (Corrette 1772, 3.)

An article in the *Encyclopédie* discusses the production of these gut strings. The author, M. de la Lande, states that the strings made by the eight *boyaudiers* in the fauxbourg Saint-Martin in Paris do not compare with those made in Naples. Therefore he travelled to Italy to research his article and at the workshop of M. Angelo Angelucci, by the fountain of serpents in Naples, he was initiated into the secrets of making the finest gut strings. Having described the ways in which the guts of seven- to eight-month-old lambs are rendered serviceable, he remarks:

> When they have been cleaned and softened for eight days in alkaline water, they are put together to be twisted; one puts only two guts together for the thinnest strings of mandolines, three for the first strings of violins, seven for the lowest. (*Encyclopédie* 1751–76, 9: 446).

Kastner records that gut e″ strings were still used on the mandoline well into the nineteenth century, and I have found no sources from this period which recommend metal top strings. Indeed Ephraim Segerman calculates that iron was not strong enough to be used at this pitch (Segerman 1986, 100). Steel of a suitable tensile strength was not developed until the second quarter of the nineteenth century,[1] when it immediately began to replace the gut strings. At baroque pitch (A–415 Hz), a gut string of about 0.5 mm is suitable. A modern nylon string of 0.6 mm is more durable, though less sonorous than gut.

Fouchetti and Corrette also give detailed information about the stringing of the lower courses:

> As regards the strings, they must be of brass. Use number 5 harpsichord strings for the a′. The d′ is number 6, but two are twisted together for each d′ ... the *bourdons* (drones), or g's, are also of gut but wound; use violin *bourdons*, but very fine ones. Some people use wound silk strings for the *bourdons*; they sound very good. (Fouchetti 1771, 5.)
>
> Harpsichord strings no. 5, yellow, for the a′, the d′ half-wound, and the g fully wound. (Corrette 1772, 3.)

French no. 5 strings at this time had a diameter of between 0.3–0.34 mm, and no. 6 strings a diameter of 0.292–0.297 mm.[2] Following Fouchetti's advice, the d′ string is produced by plaiting two no. 6 strings together into a

---

[1] Hipkins (1954) gives a fuller account of the increase in maximum string tension throughout the nineteenth century.

[2] The higher figures are given by Segerman (1986). The lower figures were given to me by Kenneth Mobbs of Bristol University.

single length. A low twist coupling has proved to be successful on the mandoline.

For the g string, an equivalent gut diameter of 1.92 mm silver-plated copper wound on gut is suitable. However these strings are noticeably lacking in high harmonics when compared to the third and second courses. It is for this reason that Fouchetti and Corrette both remark that the two fourth strings are commonly tuned an octave apart:

I have spoken of the four-string mandoline, that is to say four double strings, because they are tuned two by two in unison, that is to say to the same sound, excepting the thickest string, g, where one puts an octave. For this, use a string similar to the a′, tuned an octave above the thickest string g. Sometimes two *bourdons* are put together, then they are tuned in unison like the other three courses. (Fouchetti 1771, 5.)

Commenting on this octave tuning, Corrette declared (1772, 3) 'This tuning is the most common'. Octave stringing on lower courses was a common feature on lutes and on early guitars, as the upper string reinforced the first harmonic of the duller, thicker, gut string. If octave stringing is used, I would recommend using a slightly thicker brass string than that recommended by Fouchetti (I suggest 0.37 mm).[3]

Bortolazzi's tutor offers further information on the stringing of different types of mandolin:

There are gut strings, as on the violin, but much finer. The double wire strings, which one meets with one some mandolins, are no good; they give a far less lovely sound than the former sort ... those with eight strings are called Neapolitan; alone, these sound unpleasant, with an overly-hard, zither-like sound, so we're left as before with the newly invented four string mandolin—the Cremonese or Brescian—which is pleasing and which possesses a full songlike tone. (Bortolazzi 1805, 3.)

As we have already seen, Bortolazzi was promoting his own type of instrument at the expense of the others, so his remarks cannot be taken too seriously.

Playing Positions

The mandoline is held like the guitar with the left-hand thumb under the second course and the other four fingers rounded so as to be able to rest easily on the four courses.

---

[3] Both of Fouchetti's suggestions for the fourth course produce a tone markedly inferior to the other strings. On the advice of Ephraim Segerman I have experimented with two high twist brass strings of 0.41 mm tuned in unison (used on bandoras and orpharions until the early 17th century, but probably not manufactured in 18th century Paris) and obtained a great improvement in tone quality.

When playing while standing up it is necessary to attach a little ribbon (which ladies affix with a pin to their dress and which men slip onto a button of their coat or jacket) to a button which is behind the underside of the neck. When playing while sitting down pass the ribbon in any manner as long as the fingerboard is raised at the left side.

(Corrette 1772, 1.)

The best position for ladies, when they are seated, is to rest the body of the mandoline against the knees, towards the right side, but in such a manner that the arm does not stick out too much while one is playing. As regards men, they support the body of the mandoline against the stomach, a little on the right side and with the neck raised, as we have said.

(Fouchetti 1771, 4.)

These two descriptions are well illustrated by engravings from Denis (see Illustrations 7 and 8 above) and Leoné (Illustration 10), as well as the paintings of Lacour (Illustration 5*a*) and Tischbein (Illustration 5*b*). The two former illustrations show the common standing position, and the latter show the seated position recommended by Fouchetti. Leoné and Gervasio do not

Illustration 10. Detail from frontispiece of Leoné, *Méthode* (1768).

Illustration 11. Detail from title-page of Bortolazzi, *Anweisung* (1805).

express a preference for either position, but Bortolazzi (Illustration 11) favours the seated position for women.

Although the mandoline and violin share a common tuning, the left-hand positions for the two instruments were quite distinct. By the mid-eighteenth century, violinists had adopted the modern position with the fingers pointing towards the bridge. Mandoline technique positioned the fingers parallel with the frets, as can be seen in Illustrations 7, 8, and 10. Whereas Corrette (1772, 1) and Leoné (1768, 3) advise that the thumb should rest under the neck of the instrument (underneath the second course), violinists habitually brought the thumb around the neck. The result is that the mandoline position allows easier chordal formation (this hand position is still standard for the guitar and lute) whereas the violinist's position gives a greater facility in scale passages, especially in higher positions. Only Gervasio advocates freeing the thumb, but for an entirely different reason:

Always take note of the cross that you will find over the bass notes; they signify that on such occasions these notes must be made with the left-hand thumb, which is holding the neck of the instrument. Thus one easily manages passages which would otherwise be very difficult. (Gervasio 1767, 1.)

This fingering of bass notes with the left-hand thumb was a common eighteenth-century guitar technique. Of the mandolinists presently under discussion, only Gervasio recommends it in the text, Ex. 2 showing a passage which is simplified by this use. However, the practice was abandoned by mandolinists in general in the nineteenth century, as a hand position closer to that of the violinist was adopted.

Ex. 2

The instrument, in the sitting position, is supported at several points by the legs, the stomach, the left hand, and the right forearm. As Corrette points out: 'For the right hand to have as much liberty as possible, one must rest the forearm on the table and the elbow a little outside; not only does this give the hand a great deal of ease in giving quill strokes, but also holds the instrument against oneself.' (Corrette 1772, 1.) Leoné recommends that the forearm should rest at a point two inches from the wrist, so that the instrument is held securely in place, with the wrist free to move (Leoné 1768, 3). From all the information contained in the tutors, it seems to me that the position shown in Illustration 10 above was considered to be the most secure, the standing position being suitable for simple vocal accompaniments.

The Plectrum/Quill

The Neapolitan mandoline has always been played with a plectrum. In the eighteenth century, the modern tortoiseshell plectrum was not used, players recommending a quill instead (see Illustration 12). Ostrich feathers are advised by Leoné, but Fouchetti also suggests raven feathers, and Corrette, hen feathers. Gervasio describes the processes involved in rendering the feather serviceable:

The quill must not be stiff but, on the contrary, carved very thin. Playing imparts delicacy to it, which is the means of making a greater quantity of notes. [Thus] one makes the instrument [sound] more sweet and gracious and [through playing] one loses a sort of stiffness which it [the quill] naturally has.

One must not squeeze the string with the quill, but touch it lightly with the end of the same. The more one touches the string with delicacy, the more the sound will be melodious and pleasing.

   The quill must be cut down in this fashion until one gives it this shape, one must cut down the angles of the concave part, so that the two sides are equally flat and smooth. (Gervasio 1767, 1.)

Leoné adds some more practical advice:

It must be elastic, that is to say neither too feeble nor too stiff, otherwise one cannot give force or sweetness in playing.

   It is wrong to trim the quill when the tip has become a little wispy; a little beard is always good at least for making the notes more solemn and velvety. (Leoné 1768, 3.)

   Corrette repeats Leoné's comments and adds the following extra-musical tip to finish: 'When one has finished playing, for fear of losing the quill, put it under the strings, between the bridge and the buttons which hold the strings.' (Corrette 1772, 8.)

Plume d'Autruche ou de Corbeau .

Illustration 12. Examples of the quill, taken from the *Méthodes* of Leoné (left), Corrette (centre), and Gervasio (right). (Not to scale.)

The use of narrow quills on gut strings allows the maximum production of harmonics; after the advent of all metal stringing, wide tortoiseshell plectra were preferred as these inhibit the production of high harmonic partials and thus render the sound less 'jangly'. Although the quill was universally used in Paris, Bortolazzi preferred a small piece of cherry bark for the gut strings of his Cremonese mandolin. The Italians, he informs us, call this small plectrum *patacca* (Bortolazzi 1805, 3). Fouchetti mentions, at the very end of his tutor (1771, 18) that cherry bark should be used if the mandolin is mounted entirely with gut strings, as feathers are no good in such a case.

If one wishes to make one's own quills, I recommend cutting the feather to a length of 40–60 mm, and trimming away the barbs with a knife. It should then be filed down to about 1 mm thick, the flexibility being adjusted during play by holding it either nearer to or further from the tip. Ostrich feathers are readily obtainable from second-hand clothes' shops; one feather will provide four or five mandoline quills.

Plectrum Technique

The essence of right-hand technique on the mandoline is extremely simple: one gives either a down stroke (towards the floor) or an upstroke. These are notated in various ways by different eighteenth-century maîtres:

Maître	Downstroke	Upstroke
Gervasio	not notated	ı
Denis	not notated	ı
Leoné	\	/
Fouchetti	B (Bas)	h (haut)
Corrette	B	H
Bortolazzi	ab or .	auf or ∨

Leoné explains the difference between the down and up strokes:

the first I call *supérieur* because it is the richest and the most used . . . the second I call *inférieur* . . . this one is less sweet . . . and should not be employed except where speed demands it; it must above all be avoided in passing from a lower to a higher string because this creates the greatest difficulty. (Leoné 1768, 4–5.)

Denis attempts to simplify the rules for up and down strokes to the most basic few. Strong beats are usually played with a down stroke and one works out sequences in order to ensure this. In volume I, he applies this reasoning universally to all scales; however, in volume II (having perhaps contemplated Leoné's system and comments in the meantime) he discusses the *contre-coup de plume*. This is Denis's term for the difficulty Leoné outlined earlier of passing from a lower to a higher string with an up stroke (involving a movement with the quill away from the string one is about to play). Ex. 3, from Denis, *Méthode* (1769) illustrates manners of playing scales. Ex. 3*a* and *b* show how the *contre-coups de plume* occur; *c* and *d* show how to avoid the difficulty by use of the *coulé*. None the less, apart from certain arpeggio and *batterie* patterns (discussed later), Denis maintains that quill technique is an uncomplicated subject.

Ex. 3

By contrast, Leoné devotes a great deal of space to the matter. The mandoline, although designed in imitation of the violin, lacks the most expressive and subtle part of the resources of the latter, namely the bow. Leoné, more than any other mandolinist of the period, was acutely aware of this deficiency, and sought to develop a right-hand quill technique which would give a versatility and breadth of expression comparable to that of the violinist. In the preface to his *Méthode* he discusses the differences between plucked and bowed strings:

This instrument [mandoline], lacking a bow, is unable to sustain a note like the violin, nor can it execute a quantity of notes in a single stroke as can the latter; it has this much in common with the harpsichord and all plucked instruments. (Leoné 1768, 1.)

Having conceded these techical advantages to the violin, Leoné states that, especially in Naples where the instrument is most widely played, players have developed an exact system of signs, both to give a greater range of expression in performance, and to help with the negotiation of difficult passages. If a player does not observe these signs, Leoné warns that he or she will constantly find it necessary to consult a teacher who can demonstrate how to perform difficult passages (Leoné 1768, 20).

Besides the basic ﹨ and ╱ strokes, he gives several other ways of attacking a note. ∧ instructs the player to bend the fingers holding the quill in order to obtain a gentle attack, while ⊓ tells the player to straighten the fingers out, thus giving a firmer stroke. ∩ indicates that several notes are to be played with a single stroke of the quill. ❘ indicates an accent, a sharp dry stroke. Several other signs are also used, which will be dealt with in subsequent sections.

These are the varieties of stroking which Denis dismisses as 'a long verbiage of rules' (Denis 1768, 3). Gervasio devotes almost the whole of the text of his *Méthode* to an examination of every possible type of stroking, and Fouchetti and Corrette also put a greater emphasis on varieties of stroking than does Denis, although Leoné is alone in his use of ∧ and ⊓. One can see throughout is *Méthode Raisonnée* a desire to rationalize every aspect of his subject, a desire which dominated eighteenth-century thought in general.

The problem of stroking groups of three notes is discussed by all authors. Whereas even-numbered groups allow the use of continued up and down strokes, the triplet cannot be treated so simply. If alternate up and down strokes are used, the *inférieur* stroke will fall on the downbeat every other time, but any other system will involve at least two consecutive strokes in the same direction. One way of side-stepping the problem will be discussed later, but Gervasio summarizes the usual compromises:

Rule for triplets
When the slowness of the movement permits it, one needs to play the first of the three notes by giving a quill stroke from high to low, to give it more delicacy and grace; but when the movement is fast, they must be taken otherwise as you will see. (Gervasio 1767, 4–5)

Leoné (Illustration 6) marks out three varieties of timbre—*naturel*, *argentin*, and *fluté*. Corrette explains their function further:

One draws loud or soft sounds out according to the force that one gives to the quill strokes and according to the place on the string; where one usually plays, the sounds are drawn out below the rosette, sometimes close to the bridge, where they are tinkling, and above the rosette they are sweet and it is here that one plays piano. (Corrette 1772, 9)

Eighteenth-century mandolinists commonly equate piano and dolce, and in much mandoline music *p* and *d* are used interchangeably as contrasts to *f*.

Ornaments

Tremolo (Trill)

It is commonly stated in articles about the mandolin that tremolo, which today is an indispensable part of every mandolinist's technique, was a nineteenth-century development, rarely if ever used by eighteenth-century players. However, there is ample evidence contained in both the tutors and the music of the period to establish that this was not the case.

The various *maîtres* vary greatly in their opinions of the desirability of tremolo, or trill as it is referred to. For instance, Fouchetti describes in tones of disapproval a method of playing common amongst the Italians, and both he and Leoné recommend that the trill should be used sparingly.

There are those who trill all the notes, except for quavers and semiquavers, because there isn't time to trill those, otherwise they trill everything. In Italy one calls these sorts of mandoline players *Pétacheux*. To play the mandoline like that is like a village fiddler who plays on all the strings at once. It makes such a confusion in the harmony that one comprehends nothing. (Fouchetti 1771, 6.)

The trill, improperly so called, is a repercussion of quill strokes on the same note, which serves to sustain the duration of the note in the absence of a bow; it is useful at most only for loosening the wrist, from which I conclude that it should not be repeated too often. (Leoné 1768, 16.)

The two *maîtres* mentioned above both recommend restraint in the use of the tremolo. However other writers were more enthusiastic in advocating its use. Corrette takes a positive attitude to the technique, as an idiomatic device to be used on instruments plucked with a quill:

It has been noted that on the Mandoline one cannot swell the sound as one does with the bow on the violin. To compensate for this, one performs a *Trill* which is a repetition of the same sound on a note. The execution of the *trill* depends entirely on the right wrist. This ornament is very pretty and can only be performed on instruments which one plays with a quill such as Mandores, Mandolines, Cistres, and Turkish Vielles. The *trill*, called *Trillo* in the singular and *Trilli* in the plural by the Italians, is made on notes of long duration . . . In general, the *trill* can be made on all final notes. (Corrette 1772, 17.)

Gervasio goes further, advocating the use of tremolo on all long notes:

All single notes, for example minims, ought to be trilled. This French word, defined by M. Rousseau of Geneva, signifies here that one must agitate the string in a lively manner in opposite directions, that is to say alternately from high to low and low to high, as quickly as possible with the tip of the quill, until one has filled up the duration of the note. (Gervasio 1767, 3.)

Gervasio here is describing the non-metric tremolo, where the number and the frequency of quill strokes bears no relation to the tempo of the music. Fouchetti, Corrette, and Denis prefer a precise number of strokes in their trill as the latter *maître* explains: 'The *trille* must always have an unequal number of strokes, that is three, five, seven or more, according to the length of the note . . . the *trille* of three quill strokes is a tasteful *trille* (Denis 1768, 4). Corrette explains the reason for the insistence on the odd number of strokes:

Take care to finish with a down stroke because the *trill* is more brilliant when executed with an odd number of strokes; by this device one makes a silence of a quarter of a beat, which gives a very beautiful effect.

B H B   BHBHB

BHBHBHB   (Corrette 1772, 17.)

Denis remarks that the *trille* is used only for longer notes and must be added to the notated music principally when playing transcriptions:

One can do without *trilles* in playing music by mandolinists, because they do not use longer notes; but in other music, where long notes are employed, one must substitute and multiply with other notes, to fill the value of the long notes which the composer demands. The *trille* supplies this; and, when it is performed with a supple wrist, it is most agreeable. (Denis 1768, 5.)

From the numerous quotations given above, one can see that the tremolo was part of the technique of all the Parisian maîtres. It is often indicated in mandoline music by the sign ᷃, but more frequently left to the player's taste and discretion. In the *méthodes* the tremolo is frequently notated in full, see Ex. 4 from Leoné *Méthode* 1768, which contradicts Campbell's assertion, (1980, 609) that Grétry's use of the technique (see Ex. 5, 'Tandis que tout

Ex. 4

Ex. 5

sommeille' from *L'Amant jaloux*) is 'unusual for such an early period'. Bortolazzi also mentions the tremolo (which he terms *bebung*[4] and indicates) but his single-strung Cremonese mandolin is less suited to the technique than double-strung Neapolitan instruments.

In conclusion, it is obvious that the tremolo style of playing was well known in the eighteenth century, and practised by the *Pétacheux* in Italy.

---

[4] Wölki (1984, 15) is incorrect to say that Bortolazzi 'does not even mention the tremolo'. The reference is on p. 23 (Bortolazzi 1805).

However, these players (presumably street musicians) do not appear to have bequeathed any notated compositions to posterity. Classical players in the salons of Europe used the technique sparingly, although, from the evidence of the *méthodes* themselves, it was amongst the variety of ornaments to be introduced *ad libitum* by performers, especially to prolong the last note of a phrase.

Cadence

As we have seen above, mandoline *maîtres* used the word *trille* or *trillo* to describe the tremolo (incorrectly, as Leoné notes). The modern trill was referred to by them (with the exception of Denis as we shall see later) as a *cadence*, because it tended to occur on the penultimate note of a phrase.

Corrette (who was principally a keyboard player) uses the standard mid-eighteenth-century notation *t* for the *cadence* but both Leoné and Fouchetti prefer + , reserving *t* for tremolo.[5] Denis, in the first part of his *Méthode* refers to 'another species of *trille*' (that is, besides tremolo) which consists of four notes, starting above the main note. By extending this, he tells us, the *cadence* is formed. In the next volume he explains the execution of the *cadence*:

This is performed as on the violin, by lowering and raising the finger, through a gradation of speed, on the note above that on which [the *cadence*] is placed; but it must be noted that, at each lowering and raising of the finger, there must be a quill stroke which strikes exactly together with the finger, and that the quill must not press too hard upon the string; whereas on the violin a single bow-stroke serves for all the beatings of the finger: this makes the *cadence* easier on that instrument than on the mandoline. (Denis, 1769, 2–3.)

Corrette echoes this last remark:

Of all the ornaments the *Cadence* is the most difficult and the most necessary to be studied. One must not delude oneself into thinking right away that one can perform it well but with time one will achieve it. (Corrette 1772, 16.)

And Fouchetti considers it to be suitable only rarely on the instrument: '*Although *cadences* are scarcely practicable on the mandoline, one can however play some in certain passages'. (Fouchetti 1771, 17.)

---

[5] Gervasio does not discuss the *cadence*; instead, as seen in Ex. 2, he uses + to indicate a note fretted with the left-hand thumb.

Every tutor stresses that each note in the *cadence* must be plucked with the quill. Whereas on the guitar the left hand could be used to prolong the *cadence*, on the mandoline, the string length was considered too short (and the tension too high) for the strings to be able to absorb sufficient energy from the left-hand fingers alone to keep in full vibration.

The purpose of the *cadence* is to create greater tension (through acceleration and dissonance) before the final resolution and mandolinists developed a standard cadential formula (Fouchetti's is illustrated in Ex. 6):

One will remember to *trill* [tremolo] every time the note after the *cadence* and to *trill* it in proportion to the length [of the *cadence*]. (Fouchetti 1771, 17.)

Chords [of 3 or 4 notes] give a beautiful effect at the finale, and at the end of a melodic phrase. If, at the final note, one is unable to play a perfect *accord*, one puts a *trill* in its place [⌁], otherwise it would be too meagre, given that the mandoline cannot swell the sound as can a violin. (Corrette 1772, 25.)

Ex. 6

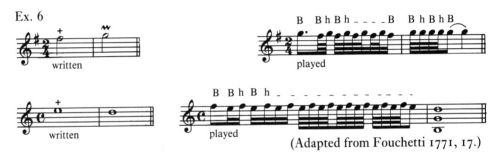

(Adapted from Fouchetti 1771, 17.)

Left-hand Techniques

Eighteenth-century mandolinists sought various ways to compensate for their instrument's weakness *vis-à-vis* the violin, in particular the latter's ability to execute many notes under a single bow stroke. On a modern high-tension mandolin it is not possible to sound notes with the left hand alone in normal circumstances (only acciaccaturas and specialist pizzicato effects are nowadays performed in this manner), but this was not the case on early instruments. As we have already seen, these were of light construction (this lightness was enhanced on the best instruments by fluting the ribs) and were strung with a gauge lighter than that used on the violin. The *cadence* was considered to be too extended an ornament to be executed adequately by the left hand alone but the following techniques are commonly employed in mandoline music of this period.

Chûte

This is the same technique as that found in Elizabethan lute music, where it is termed 'a fall'. Corrette gives a straightforward explanation:

The fall is made when there are three or four notes to play on the same string by giving only one quill stroke downwards for the 1st note and by letting the fingers fall onto the vibrating string for the other notes, without giving any more quill strokes.

(Corrette 1772, 14.)

A little later Corrette remarks that when a *chûte* is well executed, the fingers fall firmly onto the strings 'as though each finger were a little hammer'.

All the other descriptions of this technique are similar. Leoné (1768, 8) mentions that the term is taken from guitar terminology and that it is a way of sweetening the tone of the instrument and making one's playing more brilliant and agreeable. The slur over the notes of the *chûte* has a special meaning for plucked-string players, indicating that all the notes are to be played with one right-hand stroke. Thus the slur is also found in the next technique to be discussed.

Tirade

This is a reverse *chûte* and, as the name implies, the string is pulled with the left-hand fingers as Corrette describes:

The *tirade* is performed by the fingers of the left hand pulling the string with the finger above appropriate to each note, that is to say that in the example below it is necessary to pull the g with the finger that made the a, pull the f with the finger that made the g and the e with the finger that is leaving the f . . . The *tirade* is the opposite of the *chûte*, the latter is made when the notes ascend and the former when they descend. Neither can be played when one passes from one string to another.

(Corrette 1772, 15.)

Although Corrette prefers to mark the *tirade* with a succession of Ts, other *maîtres* use the slur exactly in the same way as with the *chûte*. Indeed both these techniques can be seen as varieties of the *coulé*.

Coulé

This liaison ⌒ which one often finds above notes shows that those notes which are thus tied must be made with the quill from high to low [that is, with one continuous down stroke].

(Gervasio 1767, 1)

The above example is played by fingering the d on the fourth string, the f on the third, and the a on the open second, and then allowing the quill to flow over the strings in one continuous down stroke (hence the name: *couler* means to flow).

   Corrette uses the term in a more general manner to describe all ways of playing more than one note per quill-stroke:

One plays *notes coulées* with the same stroke of the quill. When there are bindings A ⌒ E on two or three notes one plays them with a single stroke of the quill. A greater quantity [of notes] will not be heard: it's not the same as the violin where one can bind together a dozen notes under a single bow stroke. (Corrette 1772, 12.)

Indeed Corrette also applies the term to a variety of *petites notes* performed with the left hand, as the next section describes.

Petites Notes

These would nowadays be called acciaccaturas, but Leoné and Denis use the above term, while Fouchetti and Corrette subdivide them further into *port de voix* and *coulé*.

   In eighteenth-century treatises (and commentaries upon them ever since), a great deal of space is devoted to the performance of 'little notes'. C. P. E. Bach (Berlin, 1759, 87) for example, observes that 'In execution some appoggiaturas vary in length; others are always rapid', and it is frequently difficult to ascertain which is which. However this problem does not arise in mandoline music for the simple reason that *petites notes* are always played in the *coulé* manner described above, and that this technique is applicable only to ornaments of very brief duration. Leoné describes their execution, linking them with the falling and pulling techniques discussed earlier.

There are two types of *petites notes* ... The first which ascends is made by giving a strong down stroke with the quill and letting the following finger fall immediately after, the two sounds being made together with a single stroke. This is called *chûte* on the guitar.

The second which descends is pulled with the finger above the main note, unlike the first, and it is this which is called *tirade* on the guitar.

                    (Leoné 1768, 13.)

Corrette and Fouchetti separate the two species by their common musical names; the *port de voix* and the *coulé* (yet another nuance of meaning for this word!). As Corrette points out:

The *port de voix* ... is similar to the *chûte*: the difference consists only in the number of notes, given that in the *chûte* one performs many notes without giving quill strokes, and that for the *port de voix* one makes only one on the vibrating string. (Corrette 1772, 18.)

He also notes that these ornaments are scarcely ever performed on the fourth string; although he gives no reason, it presumably lies in the octave stringing. The thick g and thin g′ strings would not react equally to the pulling of left-hand fingers and thus this technique would be better avoided.

As for the use of appoggiaturas, these ornaments were written as ordinary large notes. The small note tied to the large was reserved (whether on violin, voice, or mandoline) to indicate two notes performed with a single attack. As long appoggiaturas required a stroke on the *petite* and main notes, mandoline *maîtres* considered it preferable to indicate both notes in full.

Batterie

One calls *Batteries* two notes on different degrees struck one after the other several times; when the notes are on two different strings the effect is more beautiful.

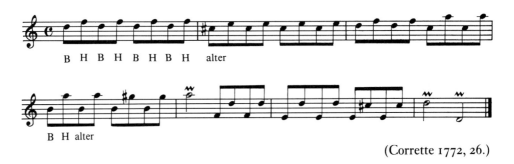

(Corrette 1772, 26.)

The following sections will discuss various ways of prolonging sounds on the mandoline. As noted earlier, the *trille* was not considered by many of the Parisian *maîtres* to be suitable for constant usage. Amongst the alternatives was the *batterie*. This is of course a standard formula on all instruments but, as Corrette remarks, when performed on the mandoline on two different courses it has a particularly full sound. This is because the two courses ring on in between strokes, giving the effect of interlocking tied crotchets. Indeed, according to Denis, this is the essence of the technique:

Batteries are quantities of pairs of notes, where the first is on one string and the second on another continuing the same as the following example; when the first of the two notes is the lower, the quill stroke is down, and up for the second note; but when the first of the two is the higher, the quill stroke is up and that of the second note is down.

(Denis 1768, 9.)

Note that in this last example the quill-stroking at *b* is the reverse of the usual sequence, with the weaker up stroke falling on the beat. This allows each stroke to be performed in such a way that the follow-through brings it into a position where it is ready to attack the next note; if the normal down/up pattern was preserved, the quill would have to be brought back over the string just played before the next note could be executed.

Arpeges

This technique allowed the *maîtres* to show off their brilliance with different *coups de plume*. Indeed Denis considered them so idiosyncratic that he identified certain patterns with certain Neapolitan virtuosos (Illustration 13). Leoné devotes a full page of his *Méthode* to an exhibition of twenty varieties of three-course *arpeges* (Illustration 14), suggesting that when an arpeggio passage is encountered in a piece, the player should choose a suitable pattern from the *magazin*. Corrette notes that, although a composer will usually indicate how he wishes arpeggio passages to be performed (by writing out the first measure in full, and subsequent bars as chords), the player is often free to interpret such passages *ad libitum*.

Customary rules of stroking are often set aside in the execution of *arpeges*.

(continued)

Illustration 13. Denis: favourite *coups de plume* of the *maîtres*. (1768, 9–10.)

Use is made of the *coulé* technique, gliding the quill over the strings in one continuous down or up stroke. Gervasio for instance gives a most unconventional stroking for the *arpege* (see Ex. 7); the three-note downbeat chord is played with an up stroke and the next three semiquavers played *coulé* with a single down stroke. In *arpege* playing, as with the *batterie*, facility of execution is primary to observation of the normal rules of stressed and weak beats.

Ex. 7

14 *Magazin*

De differents mouvements de plume, où les doigts restant toujours dans la même place
la forcent à travailler de plusieurs façons; ce qui est de la plus grande utilité pour se
rendre Maître de tous les mouvements desquels depend la plus difficile execution,
je conseille à ceux qui voudront profiter de cette regle de s'y execcer jusqu'à
ce qu'une de ces manieres d'arpêger leur soit bien familiere avant que de
passer à une autre, et quand ils les possederont toutes, ils pourront se flatter
d'être très habiles Na les Cases marquées d'un * se rassemblent entr_elles
pour les coups de plume

n.a. Je ne parlé — pas des Arpéges a 4 Cordes
puis qu'ils se trouvent tacitement renfermés dans des coups de plume
qui sont marquée ci deffous

Illustration 14. Leoné; varieties of *arpege*. (1768, 14.)

Martellement

Corrette and Leoné suggest this left-hand ornament as another means of prolonging a note:

The *Martellement* can be made before a long note:

this ornament is composed of three *petites notes*, made with the same quill stroke. One can also execute it by beating the fingers one after another on the string as rapidly as possible, in which case one gives a quill stroke only on the minim note. (Corrette 1772, 20.)

Jouer la blanche

As remarked earlier, Leoné disliked extensive use of the *trille* as a means of prolonging a note. In place of this he considers other ways of prolonging a minim (*blanche*) illustrated in Ex. 8:

Ex. 8

Instead of using a *trille* to fill the minim, I find it more agreeable to make a cadence by dividing it into two crotchets, playing a *martellement* on each. One can also use ornaments, be they *petites notes* or other harmony notes, the whole being done in accordance with the knowledge and ability of the player. NB One can also divide it with the octave in the bass. (Leoné 1768, 17.)

By *cadence* Leoné here means a rhythmic construction on a note.

Only Leoné devotes a whole section of his *Méthode* to a discussion of the filling-in of long notes. However, as shown in Ex. 6 above, Fouchetti preferred to fill in pairs of long notes with a *cadence* and a *trille*, while Corrette used *accords*.

Accords

One calls *accord* two sounds struck together on two different strings with the same quill stroke, sometimes on 3 or 4 strings. These latter sorts are found very often as final notes of melodies.

(Corrette 1772, 22.)

It has already been noted that the *accord* was used as an alternative to a *trille* at the end of phrases. As with violin writing, passages of double- (and even triple/quadruple-) stopping are also commonly encountered in music for mandoline. However Corrette and Leoné both discuss a technique peculiar to the mandoline by which double-stopping can be performed on a single course:

The stringing being double and unison on the mandoline, it is possible to draw out two different sounds at once. To obtain this, one must first place the finger on the lower note, very upright on the two strings that make the unison, then place the upper note finger skilfully in such a manner that it only touches the string situated towards the lower part of the instrument.

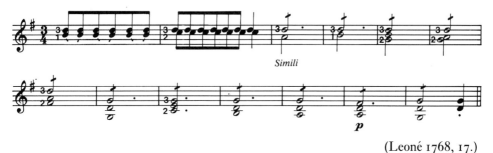

(Leoné 1768, 17.)

Corrette however, having discussed this technique, remarks upon the difficulty of executing *accords* in this manner, due to the likelihood of the upper finger fouling the lower note. He therefore recommends that the notes should be played on two different courses where possible. On modern instruments, where the two strings of each course are very close together (to allow a smoother tremolo) this technique is not considered practicable, (although scordatura is often used as a method of playing two notes on a single course).

Scordatura

The tuning of the two strings of a course to different notes allows the mandolinist to perform passages in thirds and close position chords which would
otherwise be impossible. Several eighteenth-century mandolinists took
advantage of this possibility in their compositions. Leoné hints at this in his
Méthode (p. 20): 'In the work which I will publish after this one will be
found pieces for the mandoline tuned in diverse manners.' Unfortunately no
copy of this proposed work is known. However, Antoine Riggieri uses
scordatura technique in the second movement (Adagio) of his Sonata V from
Op. 4, where one of the two unison d's is tuned to b (see Ex. 9). The piece
needs, of course, to be carefully composed and fingered if it is not to descend
into bitonal nonsense.

Ex. 9

Pietro Denis also uses this device in Prelude 7 from Part II of his
Méthode: 'The piece must be played after having tuned one of the two thirds
a tone and a half lower than the other [see Ex. 10].' (Denis 1769, 7).

Ex. 10

Although it is not clear from the *Méthodes*, my own opinion is that the
lower of the notes should be found on the string nearest to the bass, so that
when playing down strokes the two notes will be played lower/higher.

Notes inégales

The systematic execution of written quavers as alternate dotted quavers and semiquavers (a universal practice amongst French musicians of the late seventeenth and early eighteenth centuries) had begun to die out by the period of the *maîtres de mandoline* of Paris. Furthermore, only Corrette, amongst those who published tutors, was a Frenchman,[6] and Italians conventionally notated (or at least indicated) irregular rhythms in full. Therefore it is not surprising to find that only Corrette discusses the matter:

Observe that the down stroke in passing sounds both of the strings in unison whereas the up stroke sometimes only sounds one; this gives a preference to the first type for long notes. Normally in Menuets, Chaconnes, Passacailles, Sarabandes one plays the quavers *inégales* without them being dotted in the music. (Corrette 1772, 10.)

With the exception of the minuet, these are all forms associated with the baroque suite, and are not encountered in music for mandoline of this period. As regards the minuet, I believe that Corrette's remarks only apply to the French form of this dance; the minuets of the Italian maîtres are notated as the composers intended them to be played. (The *Méthodes* cover all aspects of performance so thoroughly that there seems to me to be no doubt that *notes inégales* were not discussed because this was a practice foreign to the Italian taste and considered archaic.)

Vocal Accompaniment

This instrument is very bright, it is played at night to express the painful martyrdom of lovers under the window of a mistress.

(Corrette 1772, Preface.)

Although the most enduring image of the mandolin over the past two centuries has been as the ideal instrument for serenading (in, for instance, Mozart's *Don Giovanni* and Verdi's *Otello*), only Pietro Denis of the *maîtres* presently under discussion argues in favour of its suitability for accompanying the voice. Denis devotes most of the third part of his *Méthode* (1773) to the subject, claiming that only unfamiliarity and lack of application on the

---

[6] Denis and Fouchetti may also have been Frenchmen: see Ch. 7, n. 8.

part of players limits the use of the instrument as an accompaniment to the voice:

> Often also vanity spreads the roots of ignorance, and it is this which makes many people claim even today that one cannot sing and accompany oneself on the mandoline. They even disregard the means of accomplishing it, because it requires study and application to learn. (p. 1.)

Denis, it must be mentioned, had a financial interest in the promotion of this form of music, having already published four volumes of songs with mandoline accompaniment (his arrangements of airs from the *opéra comique*) while the third part of his *Méthode* contains a fifth volume. The study and application of which he speaks refers to the method of attack to be employed. According to Denis, the strings of the mandoline must be plucked over the sound hole when the instrument is used with the voice. The resulting sound is sweet, with many of the harmonics cut out, and 'marries well with the voice' (Denis 1773, 1). Secondly the mandoline must be plucked 'at the same time as the movement of the throat which forms the sound of the voice' (Ibid.) Denis seems to be stating here that the mandoline note should be played just before the voice enters, so that the attack is not masked by the more powerful voice. The accompaniments he gives are mostly simple guitar-like arpeggios.

The difficulty with solo mandoline accompaniment to the voice is that of high tessitura. If one looks at the usage of the instrument in arias from operas of the period, such as André Grétry's *L'Amant jaloux* (1778), Giovanni Paisiello's *The Barber of Seville* (1782–4), and Antonio Salieri's *Axur* (1787), one sees that the orchestra always supplies an added bass line, giving the harmonic completion lacking from the solo instrument. The development of the bissex (see Ch. 10) in Paris *c.*1773 was an attempt (ultimately unsuccessful) to design a mandoline with the capacity to play a bass line.

Continuo Instruments

> It must be said that the mandoline and the *cistre* are never better accompanied than by the Harpsichord and the *Viole d'orphée*.
>
> (Corrette 1772, Preface.)

Although roughly half of all eighteenth-century mandolin music, whether published or manuscript, contains a bass part, none of the tutors offer any advice as to how to perform them. It is customary nowadays to assume that a keyboard realization is implied and, although very few of the bass parts are figured, this works well. Corrette (1772, 44) recommends the use of the lute stop on the harpsichord when accompanying the mandoline. There are a few Italian pieces with a full keyboard accompaniment which can be used as models.[7]

There are other possible accompaniments however. The guitar was a popular choice in Vienna *c*.1800, so it may well have been used together with mandoline in Paris twenty-five years earlier. The guitar in Paris at this time was usually a five-course instrument, lighter than the six-string instrument used in Vienna, which was closer to today's classical guitar. Another possibility is the cello, not only together with a keyboard instrument, but also as a substitute. Eighteenth-century cellists took a more harmonic approach to their instrument than today's players do, and were trained to add extra notes above the bass line which they were playing. The use of the cello is implied in Leoné's Op. II no. 2, 2nd movement (Bailleux) (see Appendix IV, Ex. 2), where the bass line is marked 'la terza corda'. The whole movement can be played on the cello G string.

Useful Addresses

Although eighteenth-century mandolines appear from time to time at auction, the majority of players will require reproduction instruments. At present very few such instruments have been built, although as demand increases I trust that more luthiers will turn their attention to the mandoline. My own Vinaccia reproduction was built by:

Wolfgang Früh
Haller Strasse 10
7182 Gerabronn
West Germany

---

[7] See for example Vincenzo Panerai's *Suonata XIV* (I:PS B199n.6.), part of which is reproduced in App. IV, Ex. 1, Bonaventura Terreni's Minuetto (I:Mc Noseda P 34. 13) and Morandi's Sonata (D-brd:B 14760).

Strings for the mandoline can be obtained, made to order, from:

Ephraim Segerman
Northern Renaissance Instruments
6 Needham Avenue
Chorlton
Manchester M21 2AA
Britain

Fascimile editions of the *Méthodes* of Leoné, Fouchetti, and Denis (bound in a single volume), of Corrette, and of the Journal de Musique are published by:

Minkoff Reprint
46, Chemin de la Mousse
1225 Chêne-Bourg
Geneva
Switzerland

A series of *Ürtext* editions of mandoline music entitled *Die Klassische Mandolin* (edited by Wilhelm Krumbach), is published by:

Joachim Trekel Verlag
Am Ohlmoorgraben 14–16
Hamburg
West Germany

Good editions are also published by:

l'Orchestre à Plectre (edited by Christian Schneider)
17 rue Saulnier
Paris 75009
France

Plucked String (edited by Neil Gladd)
P.O. Box 11125
Arlington, VA 22210
USA

Trekel, *Plucked String*, and *l'Orchestre à Plectre* all stock a wide range of mandoline publications and offer a postal service.

A further series of mandoline music (edited by Vincenz Hladky) is published by Heinrichshofen edition, Wilhelmshaven. Many of these items are in fact arrangements of mandolino music from A:Wgm, adapted to be playable on the Neapolitan instrument.

10

Instruments Related to the Neapolitan Mandoline in the Eighteenth Century

Bissex

Literally 'twice six' strings, this instrument was designed in Paris by Van Hecke and built by J. Henri Nadermann *c.*1773. It has a rounded back like a lute or mandolin, and possesses six free bass strings (A–B–c–d–e–f) which run alongside the neck, over which run a further six strings (g–a–d′–g′–b′–e″). There are twenty frets on the fingerboard.

The instrument was advertised by its inventor as being ideal for vocal accompaniments, and the six free bass strings, which give a total range of three and a half octaves, overcome the problem of high tessitura discussed earlier with regard to the mandolin. The bissex did not ever achieve widespread popularity. There is a surviving example in the Musée Instrumentale, Conservatoire de Musique, Paris. For further reading on the instrument, see Vannes (1951) and Baines (1966): the latter book contains an illustration of the *bissex* (nos. 320–1).

Colascione

The colascione was developed in Naples in the fifteenth century, probably by Turks who settled in Italy, and was a combination of the Arabian long lute (the tanbūr or buzuk), with characteristics of Italian lute construction. It is often confused with the calachon, the German name for a type of eight-course mandora, described by Albrechtsberger (1790). The overall length of the colascione was usually between 120–50 cm and the very long, narrow neck was fitted with two or three single strings, and about sixteen frets on the fingerboard.

Mersenne (1636) says that many different tunings were used but that the most common were to tune the two string version to a fifth, and the three string version to an octave and a fifth. The instrument features in many seventeenth-century Italian rustic paintings, and a smaller version, often termed the coloscioncino, achieved popularity in France in the mid-eighteenth century. It was introduced there by two Neapolitans, the Merchi brothers, in 1753, one of whose performances was commented upon by the Duc de Luynes in his *Mémoires* written in the same year:

13 June, Versailles ... At the end of the concert, two Italians played on an unusual instrument; it was a type of guitar with a very long neck. This instrument is called the *calichonchini*; it has two strings, tuned a fourth apart; it has two octaves; the strings are plucked with a small piece of tree bark, shaped to a point. They played a piece of music which was a dialogue in duo form; they got the best from their instrument, and played it most agreeably; their execution was prodigious; but one could well imagine that it is only in quick music that they could succeed. (Luynes 1860; repr. 1970, 157–8)

In an announcement for a concert he was giving at Hickford's Rooms in London in 1766, Giacomo Merchi stated that he would 'perform several pieces on a new Instrument invented by him called the Liutino Moderno, or the Calisoncino'. (Elkin 1955, 46.)

A few pieces of music for the instrument survive, including six sonatas by Domenico Colla (Dresden). For further reading on the colascione, see Donald Gill's article on the subject in *New Grove Dictionary of Musical Instruments* (1984). See also Chapter 5, 'Mandora', for details of the calachon.

Cremonese Mandolin

Bortolazzi's *Anweisung* (Leipzig, 1805) refers to this instrument as the Cremonese or Brescian mandolin, and describes it as possessing four single gut strings. The tuning was identical to that of the Neapolitan instrument, but the Cremonese mandolin had a fixed bridge like the mandolino, and a scrolled rather than a block head. The strings were plucked with a cherry-bark plectrum.

This instrument was probably developed in Cremona in the late eighteenth century (Bortolazzi speaks of it as a 'newly invented instrument'), and enjoyed a modest popularity in Vienna. There is an illustration of the instrument on the title-page of the *Anweisung* (see Illustration 11). There is an anonymous Cremonese mandolin (Italian, *c.*1810, catalogue no. I.8) in the Bach Haus, Eisenach.

Genoese Mandolin

A manuscript, attributed to Francesco Conti (a descendant of the musician mentioned at the beginning of Chapter 8) and entitled 'l'accordo della Mandola è l'istesso della Chitarra alla francese SCOLA del Leutino, osîa Mandolino alla Genovese' (*c.*1770–80), can be found in GB:Ge. Illustration 15 reproduces a depiction of a Genoese mandolin from this work. Although

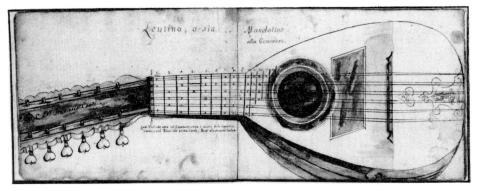

Illustration 15. Conti (attrib.), *l'accordo della Mandola*.

it gives little direct information to the mandolinist, being mostly concerned with a general explanation of musical signs and terminology, it does give the tuning of the instrument: e–a–d′–g′–b′–e″, exactly one octave above the modern guitar, and not the g–b–e′–a′–d″–g″ suggested by Sachs (1913). It should be noted that, although Sachs presumably found examples of the many different types of mandolin he lists (Fiorentino, Genovese, Padovano, Senese, etc.), there is no evidence that these existed as individual types, with the tunings he suggests, in the eighteenth century.

The following pieces by Niccolò Paganini were composed for the Genoese mandolin: 'Sonata p rovene di Niccolò Paganini' (I:PAc); 'Minuetto p l'amandorlino di Niccolò Paganini' (I:Bc); and 'Serenata p l'amandolino e chitarra francese di Niccolò Paganini' (I:Gi (l)). The three Sonatas of Zaneboni in D-ddr:SWL (listed in Appendix I) may also be intended for the Genoese mandolin rather than the mandolino, although several chords appear to have been adapted by the copyist for mandoline.

Mandola

In Part I it was noted that several different instruments have, at various times, been called mandola.[1] Most of these instruments are either of the mandolino or liuto type. Another instrument called by this name, which is still in widespread use today, is a larger version of the mandoline, tuned either c–g–d'–a' (tenor mandola) or G–d–a–e' (octave mandola).[2] It is not known whether these tunings were in use in the eighteenth century as no music or tutors for the instrument have survived.

Mandolone

To the modern mandolinist the term mandolone refers either to the mandocello (tuned C–G–d–a) or to a three-string bass instrument developed in the late nineteenth century to complete the mandolin family and to play the bass line in mandolin orchestras. However to most organologists the name refers to an eight-course instrument developed by the Roman luthier Gaspar Ferrari in the mid-eighteenth century and tuned F–G–A–d–g–b–e'–a' (see Godwin 1973).

The earliest surviving music designated for the mandolone is to be found in the Národní Muzeum in Prague, where several manuscript chamber works contain parts for the instrument (see Appendix III). However, these parts resemble cello writing, being entirely single notes, without the frequent chords one might expect in music written for an eight-course instrument. The lower range descends to C, and it may be that the intended

---

[1] Leoné (1768) notes that this confusion existed in his own day (see Ch. 6).

[2] As mentioned in Ch. 6, the earliest known instrument bearing the characteristics of the Neapolitan mandoline is a mandola by Gaetano Vinaccia, dated 1744.

instrument for these parts was actually a large mandola or mandora of the type described in Ch. 5. These Prague manuscripts also contain the earliest known use of the word mandolone.

The earliest surviving music for mandolone may well be found in a Neapolitan manuscript of *c*.1760, 'Chitarra a penna/Leuto con l'ottava' (I:Mc Noseda 48/A). The music in this manuscript is unequivocally for an eight-course plectrum instrument and as, even in the nineteenth century, the mandolone was usually referred to as the liuto, an instrument of the Ferrari type may well have been intended. The earliest surviving mandolone of which I am aware is by Gaspar Ferrari, Rome, 1744 in the Musikhistoriches Museum, Copenhagen (Claudius 133).

Appendix III

List of Primary Music Sources for the Neapolitan Mandoline*

This list comprises printed and manuscript music for mandoline(s) composed between *c*.1760–*c*.1800. It includes chamber and concerted music for the instrument, and songs with mandoline accompaniment. Some arias with mandoline accompaniment from oratorios and operas are also included. The standard RISM location symbols are used, as in the list in Appendix I. Manuscripts are further identified by shelf numbers whenever possible. Where possible, approximate dates for manuscript collections have been given.

Printed music has been dated from announcements in various eighteenth-century journals. The great majority of this music was published in Paris, and the following Parisian publications were consulted: *Annonces, affiches et avis divers, Almanach musical, l'Avant-coureur des spectacles, Avis divers, Journal de musique, Journal de Paris, Mercure de France*. Many of the publications listed are known by title only, there being no known surviving copy. However, I have included all known publications in the list, both in order to give a full picture of mandoline activity in Paris, and because I hope that copies of many of these works will be located in the future. Manuscript music has been located by a variety of means; firstly, personal searches conducted in European libraries whenever possible; secondly, a consultation of library catalogues in print; thirdly, reference to articles containing lists of mandoline music from the eighteenth century; and fourthly, from correspondence carried on with many librarians and mandolinists throughout the world during the past five years.

In some cases it has not proved possible to determine whether music is

* My Doctoral thesis, *A History of the Neapolitan Mandoline from its Origins Until the Early Nineteenth Century* (City University, London, 1989), contains a thematic index and full titles of all music for all types of mandolin composed before 1815.

intended for mandoline, mandolino, or perhaps both.[1] It is therefore possible that a few items listed here could have been intended for the mandolino. However, if used in conjunction with the list in Appendix I, a complete listing of all known mandolin music composed before 1800 will be obtained.

Considerations of space preclude a full listing of concordances. However, a few of the most important ones can be given here.

Barbella, E.	Duetto a due Mandolini (S:Uu Gimo 13):
	1st movt.: same as 1st movt. of Teleschi's Sonatina II (Paris, 1768)
	2nd movt.: same as Riggieri's Op. 1, Duetto V (Paris, *c*.1781–3)
	4th movt.: same as 2nd movt. of Giuliano's Concerto (F:Pn L2774) and 2nd movt. of Barbella from *Les Petites Récréations*, vol. 3, No. 2 (Paris, 1764)
Barbella, E.	Sonata a due Mandolini (S:Uu Gimo 14): same as
Barbella, E.	Sonata â due Madolini (F:Pn L2601)
Gaudioso, D.	Concerto di mandolino solo (S:Uu Gimo 58): same as
Gaudioso, D.	Concerto (F:Pn L2780)
Gervasio, G. B.	Sonata a Mandolino (S:Uu Gimo 141) incomplete version of
Gervasio, G. B.	Sonata per Mandolino (F:Pn L2767)
Giuliano, G.	Sinfonia per Mannolino (S;Uu Gimo 153):
	1st movt.: a complete version of
Ragiola	*Concerto di Mandolino* 1st movt. (F:Pn L2756)
Leoné,	*Six Sonates*, Op. 2 No. 6 (Paris, 1777):
	3rd movement is an arrangement of
Leoné,	*Méthode* (Paris, 1768), Duo II, 2nd movt.

[1] This is further complicated by the widespread use of 'mandolino' in Italian manuscripts, and 'mandoline' in French manuscripts, to refer to both types of mandolin. Therefore it should not be assumed from the lists in Appendix I or Appendix III that, simply because a manuscript is entitled 'sonata per mandolino', the six-course instrument is intended. In all but a few cases, original manuscripts and publications have been examined to establish to which appendix they belong.

Majo, F. de	Sonata di Mandolino e Basso (F:Pn L2757): 1st movt.: an arrangement of Teleschi's Sonatina III (Paris, 1768), 1st movt. 3rd movt.: the same as
Majo, F. de	*Les Petites Récréations*, vol. 3, No. 1 (Paris, 1764) 2nd movt.
Roëser, V.	Trio di mandolino in B♭ (F:Pn L2754): 1st and 3rd movts. same as
Roëser, V.	*Six Sonates*, Op. 3 No. 2 in C (Paris, 1769)
Ruge, F.	*Duetti* (Paris, 1768): No. 6 is the same as Veginy, *Sei duetti notturni* (Paris, 1768), Duetto V
Teleschi, A.	*Trois Sonatines* (Paris, 1768) Sonatina II, 1st movt.: same as Barbella's Duetto (S:Uu Gimo 13), 1st movt. Sonatina III, 1st Movt.: arrangement of Majo's Sonata (F:Pn L2757), 1st movt. Sonatina III, 2nd movt.: corrupted version of Barbella, *Divertimenti* (F:Pn L2613), Divertimento II, 2nd movt.

RISM SIGLA

A—AUSTRIA

A:Wgm	Vienna, Gesellschaft der Musikfreunde.
A:Wn	Vienna, Österreichische Nationalbibliothek, Musiksammlung.

B—BELGIUM

B:Bc	Brussels, Conservatoire Royal de Musique, Bibliothèque.
B:Br	Brussels, Bibliothèque Royale Albert Ier.

CS-CSSR—CZECHOSLOVAKIA

CS-ČSSR:Pnm   Prague, Národní Muzeum.

D-BRD—BUNDESREPUBLIK DEUTSCHLAND (WEST GERMANY)

D-brd:B   Berlin, Staatsbibliothek (Stiftung Preussischer Kulturbesitz).

D-brd:DO   Donaueschingen, Fürstlich Fürstenbergische Hofbibliothek.

D-brd:F   Frankfurt Am Main, Deutsche Bibliothek.

D-brd:WERl   Wertheim/Main, Fürstlich Löwenstein'sche Bibliothek.

D-DDR—DEUTSCHE DEMOKRATISCHE REPUBLIK (EAST GERMANY)

D-ddr:Bds   Berlin, Deutsche Staatsbibliothek, Musikabteilung.

D-ddr:Dlb   Dresden, Sächsische Landesbibliothek, Musikabteilung.

D-ddr:SWL   Schwerin, Wissenschaftliche Allgemeinbibliothek (Landesbibliothek).

F—FRANCE

F:LA   Laon, Bibliothèque Municipale.

F:Pa   Paris, Bibliothèque de l'Arsenal.

F:Pc   Paris, Bibliothèque Nationale (Fonds. Conservatoire).

F:Pm   Paris, Bibliothèque Mazarine.

F:Pn   Paris, Bibliothèque Nationale.

F:Po   Paris, Bibliothèque-Musée de l'Opera.

F:Psg   Paris, Bibliothèque Ste. Geneviève.

F:Pthibault   Paris, Collection Thibault (part of this collection is in F:Pn, part in private ownership).

F:TLm   Toulouse, Bibliothèque Municipale.

GB—GREAT BRITAIN

GB:Ckc	Cambridge, Kings College, Rowe Music Library.
GB:Ge	Glasgow, Euing Music Library.
GB:Lbl	London, The British Library.
GB:Ob	Oxford, Bodleian Library.
GB:P	Perth, Sandeman Public Library.

I—ITALY

I:Bag	Bologna, Biblioteca dell'Archiginnasio.
I:Bc	Bologna, Civico Museo Bibliografico Musicale.
I:Bgc	Bergamo, Biblioteca Civica Angelo Mai.
I:Bsf	Bologna, Convento di S. Francesco.
I:CORc	Correggio, Biblioteca comunale.
I:Gi(l)	Genoa, Biblioteca dell'Istituto (Liceo) Musicale 'Paganini'.
I:Ls	Lucca, Biblioteca del seminario arcivescovile presso la Curia.
I:Mc	Milan, Biblioteca del Conservatorio 'Giuseppe Verdi'.
I:MTventuri	Montecatini-Terme, private library of Antonio Venturi (now in I:MTc Montecatini-Terme, Biblioteca civica).
I:Nc	Naples, Biblioteca del Conservatorio di Musica S. Pietro a Maiella.
I:PAc	Parma, Conservatorio di Musica 'Arrigo Boito'.
I:PS	Pistoia, Archivio Capitolare del Duomo.
I:Rv	Rome, Biblioteca Vallicelliana.
I:TSmt	Trieste, Civico Museo Teatrale di fondazione Carlo Schmidl.

NL—THE NETHERLANDS

NL:DHgm	Den Haag, Gemeente Museum.

Published Music

A Chronological Listing of Instrumental Music Published in Paris 1761–83

COMPOSER	TITLE	LOCATION	DATE	REMARKS
Leoné	*30 Variations en dispute à deux violons, qui peuvent se jouer . . . sur la Mandoline*	——	1761	
Leoné	*Duo pour deux violons qui peuvent se jouer sur la mandoline* (RISM L1978 & L1979)	F:Pn, I:Nc	1762	
Various composers	*Les Petites Récréations de la Campagne, premier livre, contenant huit duetti à due violini ô Mandolini*	——	1762	
Merchi, G.	*Trios pour 2 violons ou mandolines, et violoncelle, Op. 9*	GB:Lbl	*c.*1761–4	

COMPOSER	TITLE	LOCATION	DATE	REMARKS
Various composers	*Les Petites Récréations de la Campagne, deuxième livre*	——	*c*.1763	
Denis, P.	*6 Duos pour la Mandoline*	——	1764	
Maio, Barbella, Barbella [*sic*], Giuliano, Hasse, Gaetano	*Les Petites Récréations de la Campagne, IIIe*	US:BE	1764	
Sciroli, Ragiola, Mancinelli, Barbella, Eterardi, Conforto	*Les Petites Récréations de la Campagne, IVe livre*	F:Pn	1765	
Denis, P.	*Six Sonates pour la mandoline et basse*	F:Pn	1765	
Fouquet, J.	*Six Duos pour 2 mandolines*	——	1765	
Merchi, G.	*6 Duos a deux mandolines, Op. 15*	——	1766	
Various composers	*Les Petites Récréations de la Campagne, v^e livre*	——	1766	
Leoné	*Six Sonates de Mandoline et Basse* (RISM L1977)	F:Pn	1767	
Various composers	*Les Petites Récréations de la Campagne, VIe livre*	——	1767	
Dingli, G.	*Sei Sonate à due violini, ò mandolini*	——	1767	Possibly the same work as Dingli's *Sei Sonate* of 1769 (RISM D3113)
Gervasio, G. B.	*Méthode très facile Pour apprendre à jouer de la Mandoline à quatre Cordes* (RISM G1678)	US:Wc	1767	
Miroglio	*7e suite des Amusemens des Dames, Duo pour 2 violons, mandolines ou par-dessus de viole, Op. 2*	——	1767	Suites 1–6 and 9 are not for mandoline
M * * * (Miroglio?)	*8e Suite des Amusemens des Dames, petits Airs en duo pour 2 Violons, Mandolines ou Par-dessus de viole*	——	1767	
Canabich	*6 Sonates en duo pour 2 violons, 2 par-dessus, 2 flutes ou 2 mandolines*	——	1767	
Gaëtan	*Recueil de menuets à deux mandolines*	——	1768	

COMPOSER	TITLE	LOCATION	DATE	REMARKS
Denis, P.	*Méthode Pour Apprendre à Jouer de la Mandoline* (RISM D1645)	A:Wn, F:Pn, GB:Lbl	1768	The copy in GB: Lbl contains approx. 40 pages of short manuscript dance pieces (presumably for mande.) bound in with the *Méthode*
Leoné	*Méthode Raisonnée Pour Passer du Violon à la Mandoline* (RISM L1980, L1981, L1982)	F:Pn, NL: DHgm, D-brd:DO	1768	
Various composers	*Les Petites Récréations de la Campagne livres VIIᵉ, VIIIᵉ & IXᵉ*	——	1768	
Veginy, G.	*Sei duetti notturni a flauto traverso e mandolini o due violini* (RISM V1091)	GB:Ckc, F: Pn	1768 (Lyon, 1766)	
Various composers	*Les Petites Récréations de la Campagne, Xᵉ livre*	——	1768	
Barbella, E.	*Six sonates à Violon & Basse . . . utile pour les amateurs de mandoline*	——	1768	
Teleschi, A.	*Trois Sonatines à Deux Mandolines* (RISM T458)	GB:Lbl	1768	
Anon./Bordet	*Recueil d'Airs, Ariettes, Vaudevilles, Romances . . . pour 2 violons, par-dessus de violes ou mandolines*	——	1768	
M * * * (Miroglio?)	*Xᵉ suite des Amusemens des Dames composée de plusieurs Allemandes nouvelles . . . pour 2 violons . . . ou mandolines*	——	1768	
Leoné	*Minuets pour mandoline*	——	1768	
Ruge, F.	*Duetti a due flauti traversi o due mandolini*	F:TLm	1768	
Dingli, G.	*Sei Sonate à due Violini ò Mandolini ò altri Istromenti. Dediés à Mʳ de Rochebrune* (RISM D3113)	F:Pn	1769	
Roeser, V.	*Six Sonates à deux violons et basse & qui peuvent s'exécuter sur la mandoline, Op. 3*	F:Pn	1769	

COMPOSER	TITLE	LOCATION	DATE	REMARKS
Mazzuchelli	*Un AIR connu varié . . . pour la mandoline & basse*	——	1769	
Burckhoffer	*6 Duos pour mandoline & violon*, Op. 5	——	1769	
Denis, P.	*Seconde Partie de la Méthode* (RISM D1645)	F:Pn, GB: Lbl	1769	
Fantiny	*6 Duo pour 2 violons, mandolines, ou par-dessus de violes*, Op. 1	——	1769	
Fouchetti, G.	*Sei Duetti facili per gli amatori, à due violini, o due mandolini*, Op. 2	——	1770	
Papavoine	*Recueil d'airs choisis . . . mis en Duo pour 2 violons ou mandolines*, Op. 5	——	1770	RISM P872 is not the same as this work, which was advertised in the *Journal de Musique*, Oct. 1770
Anon.	*Petite pièce de Mandoline*	——	1770	Published in the supplement to the *Journal de Musique*, Nov. 1770 (p. 8)
Anon.	*1 duo seule pour la mandoline*	——	1770 (Lyon, 1769)	
Carpentier, J.	*Méthode . . . de l'Instrument appelle Cytre*	F:Pn, F:Pm, F:Psg	1771	This contains several pieces with mande. obbl.
Fouchetti, G.	*Méthode pour apprendre facilement à jouer de la Mandoline à 4 et à 6 cordes*	F:Pn	1771	
Le Berton/Le Breton, M.	*Deuxième recueil de duo . . . arrangés pour . . . deux mandolines*	——	1771	The 1st vol. of duos were not for mande.
Fouquet, J.	*Recueil de jolis airs . . . pour deux mandolines* (RISM F1546)	NL:DHgm	1772	
Le Berton/Le Breton, M.	*3ᵉ Recueil de Duo . . . pour 2 violons, 2 mandolines ou 2 par-dessus de violes*	——	1772	
Corrette, M.	*Nouvelle Méthode Pour apprendre . . . la Madõline*	F:Pn	1772	
Fridzieri/Frixeri	*6 Sonates pour mandoline*	——	1772	

COMPOSER	TITLE	LOCATION	DATE	REMARKS
Barbella, E.	*Six Duos pour deux violons ou deux mandolines avec une basse ad. lib* . . . (RISM B884)	US:Wc, F:Pn	1772–3	The copy in F:Pn lacks the bass part
Denis, P.	*Troisième et dernière partie de la Méthode* (RISM D1645)	A:Wn	1773	
Corrette, M.	*XXIV Concerto comique . . . Accomodé pour les Violons, Flûtes, Hautbois, Par-dessus, Mandolines, Alto, avec la Basse obligée pour le Clavecin*	GB:Lbl	1773	
Leoné	*Duos pour mandoline*	——	1774	
Giuliano, G.	*Sei Sonate cantati per camera a violino & bassa osia mandolino & viola*, Op. 1	——	1776	
Cauciello, P.	*Sei Duetti per due violini, overo mandolini*, Op. 2 (RISM C1536)	F:Pthibault, D-ddr:Bds	1776	F:Pthibault lacks mande. 2 part
Mazzuchelly	*Recueil d'ariettes . . . arrangées pour deux mandolines*	F:Pn	1776	Mande. 2 part only
Lávallière	*Six Sonates en duo pour le tambourin accompagnées d'une violine seul . . . Elles peuvent s'exécuter sur le violon, flûte, hautbois, clarinette, par-dessus de viole, mandoline, guitarre, & sur la vielle & musette*, Op. 11	——	1777	
Leoné	*"Ah! vous dirai-je maman" avec 30 variations en duo pour une mandoline & un violon*, Op. 4	——	1777	Probably a repr. of an earlier work
Leoné	*Six Sonates pour la Mandoline avec la Basse*, Op. 2	GB:Lbl	1777	Probably a repr. of an earlier work. However, these sonatas are not the same as RISM L1977 in F:Pn, which were published by Bérault. The GB:Lbl sonatas were published by Bailleux (see App. IV, Ex. 2)

COMPOSER	TITLE	LOCATION	DATE	REMARKS
Gervasio, G. B.	*Six Sonates pour mandoline, ou violon & basse*	——	1778	
Fargere	*Six Sonate per il mandolino o per il Violino*	F:Pn	1778	
Mazzuchelli	*Second recueil d'airs pour mandoline & violin*	——	1778	
de Machi	*3 Trio pour deux mandolines et basse*	——	*c.*1780	
Riggieri, A.	*Six Duo à deux mandolines et Six Sonates à Mandoline et Basse*, Op. 1 (RISM R1532)	GB:Lbl, F: Pn	*c.*1781–3	Date estimated from 1783 catalogue of
Riggieri, A.	*Airs Italiens . . . et Sonates en Duo Pour la Mandoline*, Op. 2 (RISM R1533)	GB:Lbl. F: Pn	*c.*1781–3	Girard. However, in the *Affiches de Lyon*,
Riggieri, A.	*Six Duo à deux mandolines*, Op. 3 (RISM R1534)	GB:Lbl. F: Pn	*c.*1781–3	23 Dec. 1767, the music shop
Riggieri, A.	*Menuets, allemandes et petits allegro à Deux Mandolines ou violon avec six sonates à mandoline accord different*, Op. 4 (RISM R1535)	F:Pn	*c.*1871–3	Castaud announced 'many new works for clavecin, harpe,
Riggieri, A.	*La Fustemberg, Variationi Nᵒ. 10* (RISM R1536)	F:Pn, US:Wc	*c.*1781–3	guitar & mandoline by Bach, Toeschi, Pugnani, Meyer, Merchi, de Mignaux, Rigiesi, Gaëtan and others'. If Rigiesi is the same composer as Riggieri, then he was obviously active many years before the appearance of his works in Girard's catalogue.

A Chronological Listing of Music Published in Paris 1765–83 (Vocal with Mandoline Accompaniment)

COMPOSER	TITLE	LOCATION	DATE	REMARKS
Anon.	*Le Festin de l'Amour à 4 parties, voix seule, harpe, guitarre, mandoline, violons, ou clavecin et basse*	——	1765	
Anon.	*Les Projets de l'Amour avec les mêmes accompagnemens*	——	1765	
Denis. P.	*Recueil de douze petits airs . . . avec deux differens accompagnemens de mandoline* (RISM D1642)	D-brd: WERl, F: Pn	1769	
Denis, P.	*Second recueil de petits airs . . . avec accompagnement de Mandoline, et les Folies d'Espagne, avec des variations faciles* (RISM D1643)	D-brd: WERl, F: Pn, S: Skma	1770	Contains instrumental music
Cramer, W.	*Petit air de M' Cramer*	——	1770	Voice with mande. acc. Appeared in the supplement to the *Journal de Musique*, June 1770 (pp. 4–6)
Framery, N.	*Romance: 'Le tems n'est plus'*	——	1770	Voice with mande. acc. Appeared in the supplement to the *Journal de Musique*, Aug. 1770 (pp. 5–6)
Denis, P.	*Troisième Recueil de petits airs . . . avec accompagnement de mandoline* (RISM D1644)	D-brd: WERl, S: Skma, F: Pn	1770	
Cifolelli, G.	*Ah! laisse-moi, Lucas*	——	1770	Voice with mande. and basso. Appeared in the supplement to *Journal de Musique*, Sept. 1770 (pp. 5–10)

COMPOSER	TITLE	LOCATION	DATE	REMARKS
Denis, P.	*4ᵉ Recueil de Petits Airs . . . avec accompagnement de mandoline; & le Menuet d'Exaudé*	——	1770 (see no. 20)	Contains instrumental music
Denis, P.	*Les IV Saisons Européenes 1ʳ recueil*	——	1773	
Denis, P.	*Troisième et dernière Partie de la Méthode Pour apprendre à Jouer de la Mandoline . . . De plus le cinquième Recueil de petits airs* (RISM D1645)	A:Wn	1773	Contains instrumental music
Denis. P.	*Les IV Saisons Européenes 2ᵉ recueil*	B:Bc	1774	
Carpentier, J.	*IVᵐᵉ Recueil d'airs de toute espèce . . . avec Violon obligé ou Mandoline*	F:Pn, F:Pm, F:Psg, GB:Lbl, NL: DHgm	1776	
Fouchetti, G.	*Recueil d'airs choisis . . . avec accompagnement de mandoline*	——	1778–9	
Carpentier, J.	*VIIIᵉ recueil de petits airs . . . avec accompagnements obligé de . . . mandoline*	F:Pn, F:Pm, F:Psg	1780–1	
Mazzuchelli	*Troisième recueil d'ariettes choisis, avec accompagnement de mandoline*	——	1783	
Nonnini, G.	*Six Ariettes italiennes . . . qui peuvent accompagnés avec . . . mandoline*	——	1783	

London Publications

COMPOSER	TITLE	LOCATION	DATE	REMARKS
Anon.	*Eighteen Divertimentos for two Guitars or two Mandelins*	GB:Lbl, GB: Ob, GB:P, US:IO	1757	
Anon.	*Country Dances for the Violin, Mandolin . . . Composed by an African*	GB:Lbl	*c*.1775	The African was probably Ignatius Sancho

COMPOSER	TITLE	LOCATION	DATE	REMARKS
Gervasio, G. B.	*Airs for the mandoline, guittar, violin* (RISM G1679)	GB:Lbl	*c.*1768	This item is presently missing
Gualdo, G.	*Six Easy Evening Entertainments for Two Mandolins or Two Violins with a Thorough Bass for the Harpsichord*, Op. 3	GB:Ckc	*c.*1765	
Leoné	*A complete introduction to the art of playing the mandoline*	GB:Lbl, GB: Ob, US: Wc, US: NYp	1785	A trans. of the Paris edn., published in London by Longman & Broderip
Nonnini, G.	*Six Italian Canzonettes for a single voice which may be accompanied either by the Harpsichord, Guitar, Harp or Mandolin*, Op. 1	I:Bc	*c.*1785	Probably a republication of Nonnini's *Six Ariettes Italiennes* (Paris, 1783)
Mussolini, Cesare	*Six New Songs and Six Minuets . . . adapted for yᵉ guittar & Mandolin*	GB:Lbl	*c.*1790	

Other Publications

COMPOSER	TITLE	LOCATION	DATE	REMARKS
Colizzi, J. A. K.	*Airs choisis des opéras français, accomodés pour deux violons ou deux mandolines*	D-brd:F	La Haye, *c.*1785	
Colizzi, J. A. K.	*Concerto in D a violino concertante o mandolino, due violini di ripieno, violetti, due corni ad libitum e basso* (RISM CC 3365a)	S:Smf	Den Haag, *c.*1785	
Déduit	*Couplets à une Dame très aimable avec accompagnement de Mandoline ou de Violon pizzicato. Air Daigne écouter ['A qui vous voit gare cette blessure']*	F:LA	(?)	

COMPOSER	TITLE	LOCATION	DATE	REMARKS
Gervasio, G. B.	*Sei duetti per due mandolini,* *Op. 5* (RISM G1680)	I:TSmt	Vienna, *c.*1786	
Panerai, Vincenzo	*Suonata Decimaquarto per* *Cimbalo a Pianoforte e* *Mandolino o Violino* *obbligato* (RISM P843)	I:PS	Florence, *c.*1780	

Manuscript Collections

Location: A:Wgm[1]

COMPOSER	TITLE	SHELF NO	REMARKS
Giuliani, G. F.	VI Quartetti per Mandolino, Violino e Violoncello ò Viola e Liuto	X19761 (Q16845)	
Kozeluch, L.	Concertant	VII 15407	For vns. 1 and 2, vas., 2 obs., 2 hns. in E♭, 2bns., mande., 2 tpts. in E♭, contrabass, pf., and basso

Location: CS-ČSSR:Pnm[2]

Anon.	Divertissement	Lxxxii A 98	For mandolino, violino, and mandolono
Anon.	Terzetto in A per il Mandolino con Violino e Mandolone	Lxxxii A 269	Composed for Leonardi Dont
Anon.	Terzetto in B a Mandolino Violino e Mandolone	Lxxxii A 270	Composed for Leonardi Dont
Anon.	Terzetto in C a Mandolino Violino e Mandolone	Lxxxii A 271	Composed for Leonardi Dont

[1] These MSS date from *c.*1800.

[2] The MSS with bowed strings date from *c.*1790.

COMPOSER	TITLE	SHELF NO	REMARKS
Anon.	Terzetto in F a Mandolino Violino e Mandolone	Lxxxii A 276	Composed for Leonardi Dont
Anon.	Terzetto in D a Mandolino Violino e Mandolone	Lxxxii A 277	Composed for Leonardi Dont
Anon.	Divertimento in Dis a Mandolino Violino e Mandolono	Lxxxii A 419	
Anon.	Divertimento in G a Mandolino Violino e Mandolone	Lxxxii A 422	Composed for Leonardi Dont
Anon.	Trio in C a Mandolino Violino e Mandolono	Lxxxii A 440	
Anon.	Fundamentum	XLII A 136	
Anon.	March	XLII A 117	
Arauhal, B.	Quadro in Dis[,] N. 6[,] a Mandolino Violino Alto Viola con Violoncello	Lxxxii A 16	
Arauhal, B.	Quadro in B[,] N. 5[,] à Mandolino Violino Alto Viola con Violoncello	Lxxxii A 17	
Arauhal, B.	Quadro in C[,] N. 4[,] a Mandolino Violino Alto Viola con Violoncello ·	Lxxxii A 18	
Arauhal, B.	Quadro in D♮[,] N. 3[,] per il Mandolino Violino Alto Viola con Violoncello	Lxxxii A 19	
Arauhal, B.	Quadro in F[,] N. 2do[,] per il Mandolino Violino Alto Viola con Violoncello	Lxxxii A 20	
Arauhal, B.	Quadro in G[,] N. 1mo[,] per il Mandolino Violino Alto Viola con Violoncello	Lxxxii A 21	
Arauhal, B.	Cassatione in B. Mandolino violino viola 1mo viola 2da con violoncello	Lxxxii A 316	
Barbella, E.	Divertimento in A a Due Mandolini e Mandolono	Lxxxii A 418	
Call, L. de	Variations	XLII A 30	
Dussik, J. L.	Quartetto in F a Mandolino Violino Alto Viola con Mandolono	Lxxxii A 584	
Dussik, J. L.	Quartetto in G a Mandolino Violino Alto Viola con Mandolono o Violoncello	Lxxxii A 585	
Grenser	Divertimento in C per il Mandolino Violino e Mandolono	Lxxxii A 282	

COMPOSER	TITLE	SHELF NO	REMARKS
Leoné	Duetti in G. à Mandolino Primo. Mandolino Secondo	XLII A 110	
Leoné	Duetti, per due Mandolini	XLII A 115	A copy of Duo I from Leoné's *Méthode* (Paris, 1768)
Leoné	Divertimento in B a Mandolino Primo. Mandolino Secondo. Ballet Anglois.	XLII A 304	
Megelin	Divertimento in G. a Mandolino. Violino. e Mandolono.	Lxxxii A 421	

Location: D-brd:B

Morandi	Sonata Per Cembalo con acompagno di Flauto o Mandolino	14760	

Location: D-ddr:Bds

Greggio, Ignazio Secondo	6 notturni a 2 mandolini e basso	Mus. ms. 30135	Possibly now in D-brd:B

Location: D-ddr:Dlb

Vanhall, J. B.	Divertimento in C a Mandolino Violino e Mandolono.	Mus. 3417-V-1	

Location: F:Pa

Anon.	Sonatina per mandolino e cimbalo	Ms. 6785, fo. 199b	

Location: F:Pc/F:Pn[3]

Anon.	Sonata a Mandolino Solo con Basso	L2770	
Anon.	Sonata Per Mandolino e Basso	L2614	

[3] These MSS date from *c.*1764–8.

COMPOSER	TITLE	SHELF NO	REMARKS
Anon.	Duetto. Mandolino Primo	L2771	For 2 mandes.
Anon.	Duetto per due mandolini. Mandolino Primo	L2790	
Anon.	Duetto per 2 Mandolini. Mandolino Primo	L2777	
Anon.	Mandolino I:º Mandolino II:º	L2772	
Anon.	Pastorale a due mandolini è basso— Mandolino Primo	L2778	
Anon	Concerto per mandolino solo con violini e basso	D11738	For 2 vns. and basso
Anon.	Concerto à mandolino solo con violini, e basso	L2598	For 2 vns. and basso
Anon.	Concerto per mandolino, violini e basso	L2848	Vn. 1 and basso parts missing
Barbella, E.	Concerto a dui Violini, Mandolino e Basso	L2584	
Barbella, E.	Sonata â due madolini	L2601	
Barbella, E.	Divertimenti a due Mandolini ò violini	L2613	Most of the mande. 1 part for Divertimento I is missing
Barbella, E.	Sonata a Due Mandolini	L2641	
Cantone, C.	Concerto a piu stromenti per il mandolino	L2599	For 2 vns. and basso
Cantone, C.	Minuetti . . . Mandolino Primo	L2600	For 2 mandes.
Cecere, C.	Concerto per il Mandolino con dui violini e basso	L2762	The basso part is missing, as is the vn. 1 part for the 1st movt.
Cecere, C.	Divertimento di Camera di Mandolino e basso	L2761	
Cecere, C.	Divertimenti a due mandolini	L2618	
Cecere, C.	Sinfonia a due mandolini e basso	L2617	
Cecere, C.	Sonata di Mandolino solo e basso	L2763	
Cecere, C.	Sonata à Due Mandolini o Violini e Basso	L2760	
Cedronio, Duca	Divertimenti a due Mandolini	Ms. 1. 127	12 divertimenti
Cedronio, Duca	Duo a deux mandolines	L2785	There was probably an original bass part, as the 2 mandes. seem incomplete by themselves
Chiesa, M.	Suonatta a due Mandolini e Basso	L2796	

COMPOSER	TITLE	SHELF NO	REMARKS
Chiesa, M.	Notturno	L2764	Mande. 1 part missing; mande 2 and basso parts present
Cifolelli, G.	Noturno Per Mandolino e Basso	L2784	
Conforto, N.	Concerto di Mandolino con due violini e basso	L2765	
Eterardi	Sinfonia a due Violini, Mandolino & Basso	L2787	Vn. 1 part marked 'fin 1764'; vn. 2 part missing
Eterardi	Concerto a due Violini, Basso e Mandolino obligato	L2789	
Eterardi	Ouvertura a 2 Mandolini e Basso	L2788	
Gaudioso, D.	Concerto	L2780	For 2 vns. and basso.
Gervasio, G. B.	Sonata per Mandolino e Basso	Ms. 2082	'Originale' has been written in the top left-hand corner
Gervasio, G. B.	Sonata Per Mandolino solo, e Basso	L2767	
Gervasio, G. B.	Sonata Per Mandolino solo, e Basso	L2768	
Giuliano, G.	Capricio di Mandolino e Basso	L2792	
Giuliano, G.	Duetto	L2769	For 2 mandes.
Giuliano, G.	Trio a 2. Mandolini e Basso	L2773	
Giuliano, G.	Concerto Per il Mandolino con 2 violini e basso	L2774	
Lamberti, L.	Concerto a Mandolino, dui Violini e Basso	L2775	
Lecce, F.	Concerto per Mandolino: con violini e Basso	L2776	For 2 vns. and basso
Lecce, F.	Sonate a solo di violino ò mandolino	L2615	Although entitled 'Sonate a solo', there seems to be a 2nd part missing. The Conservatoire catalogue lists this work under 'Cecci'
Majo, F. di	Sonata di Mandolino e Basso	L2757	
Mancinelli, D.	Duetti Mandolino Primo	L2759	12 duets. Probably composed for fl.

COMPOSER	TITLE	SHELF NO	REMARKS
Piccinni, N.	Overtura per Duè Mandolini	L2758	For 2 mandes., va. obbl., 2 obs., 2 hns., and basso. 2 tpt. parts are missing
Prota, T.	Sinfonia a 2 violino a Basso e Mandolino	L2782	There is also a part marked 'violino terzo', almost identical to vn. 1
Prota, T.	Sonata da Mandolino e basso	L2766	
Ragiola	Concerto di Mandolino con violini e basso	L2756	Mande. part missing
Roëser, V.	Trio di mandolino o Violino	L2754	For 2 mandes. and basso
Sacchini, A.	Concerto per Violini òsia Mandolini, Oboè è Viola è Corni è Basso	D11. 142	Incomplete
Salla, C.	Sonatta à due Mandolini obbligati	L2794	With basso
Salla, C.	Suonatta à dui mandolini e basso	L2795	
Sciroli, G.	Concerto per il mandolino con dui violini e basso	L2783	
Tedesco	Sonata di mandolino e basso	L2755	
Testori, C. G.	Sonatta à dui mandolini e Basso	L2781	
Toscani, A.	Sonatta à dui mandolini e basso	L2779	
Verdone	Divertimento	L2793	For 2 mandes.
Verdone	Duetto	L2791	For 2 mandes.
Verdone	Sonata di Mandolino col Basso	L2786	

Location: F:Po

Sodi, C.	Mandolines. Divertissement (1744)		Lost

Location: GB:Lbl

Beethoven, L. van	Adagio. Sonatina per il Mandolino	Add. 29801, 87	For the other Beethoven pieces, see Ch. 8, 'Prague, Vienna, and Germany'
Cocchi, G.	Coss' e sior canapiolo.	Add. 31654, ff. 117–18	For mande. or chitarra, basso, vns., va., lisetta col tamburo

COMPOSER	TITLE	SHELF NO	REMARKS
Hummel, J. N.	Concerto scritto di G. N. Hummel per Barthol: Bortolazi Maestro di Mandolino 1799	Add. 32216, ff. 117–29	

Location: I:Bag

Giuliani, G. F.	[4] Quartetti per l'Arcileuto, Mandolino, Violino e Liuto	Bentivoglio 71 & 88	

Location: I:Bc

Stabinger, Matteo	Trio	KK 121	For mande., vn., and basso

Location: I:BGc

Puppi, Antonio	Sonata VI per Mandolino, basso	Mayr NC 3.5	A set of 6 sonatas

Location: I:Bsf

Giuliani, G. F.	Mandolino Primo. Sei Duetti Notturni Per Due Mandolini		5 complete duets, and several incomplete

Location: I:CORc

Asioli, B.	Trio a mandorlino violino è basso	44–3–5	

Location: I:Gi(l)[4]

Dothel, F.	Sonata Per due Amandolini e Basso	SS.A.2.5 (G.8)	
Giuliani, A.	Concerto Per due Amandolini, e Viola, con Violini, Oboe, Corni da Caccia, due Viole e Basso	SS.B.1.5 (H.8)	
Pleyel, I. J.	Duetto Per Due Amandolini	SS.B.1.7 (H.8)	
Rolla, A.	[2] Sonata Per un Flauto, due Amandolini, una Viola	SS.B.1.1 (H.8)	Copies of the I:Ls Giuliani quartets 3 and 5 for the same combination
Salla, C.	Sonata Notturna a tre	M.5.35	5 sonatas for 2 mandes. and basso

[4] These MSS date from *c.*1790.

COMPOSER	TITLE	SHELF NO	REMARKS
Salla, C.	Sonata Notturna a tre	SC.48	2 sonatas for 2 mandes. and basso
Stamitz, K.	Duetto S^{do} . . . Per Due Amandolini	M.25	2 duets, and a third incomplete one

Location: I:Ls

Giuliani, G. F.	Sei Quartetti per due mandolini, flauto e violoncello	B 254
Giuliano, G. F.	Sei Quartetti per due mandolini, viola e liuto	B 254
Giuliani, G. F.	Sei Quartetti per due mandolini, flauto e viola	B 254

Location: I:Mc[5]

COMPOSER	TITLE	SHELF NO	REMARKS
Anon.	Follia Variazione per Mandolino (1791)	Noseda I 31.16	For mande. and basso
Anon.	Divertimenti a due Mandolini	Noseda V 50.7	
Anon.	Divertimento Per Mandolino	Noseda V.50.16	
Anon.	Sonata a solo, e Basso Per Amandolino	Noseda A 53.10[A]	
Anon.	Sonata Per Amandolino e Basso	Noseda A 53.10[B]	
Anon.	Sonatta per Mandolino Con il Suo Basso	Noseda A 53.10[C]	
Anon.	Sonata per Mandolino	Noseda A 53.10[D]	For mande. and basso
Anon.	Concertino à Due Mandolini	Noseda A 53.10[E]	
Barbella, E.	Divertimento per due mandolini	Noseda B 40.4	
Bignili, G.	Duetto a Due Mandolini, (1789)	Noseda C 42.6	
Cauciello. P.	Trio a due Mandolini e Basso	Noseda E 25.2	
Cauciello. P.	Trio Per due Mandolini, e Basso	Noseda E 25.3	
Cauciello. P.	Trio a due Mandolini e Basso	Noseda E 25.4	
Cauciello. P.	Trio a due Mandolini e Basso	Noseda E 25.5	
Cauciello. P.	Trio Per due Mandolini e Basso	Noseda E 25.6	
Cedronio, Duca	Trio a due Mandolini e Basso (1789)	Noseda M 24.8	

[5] These MSS were probably copied *c*.1790, although much of the music dates from *c*.1762–70.

COMPOSER	TITLE	SHELF NO	REMARKS
Cedronio, Duca	Trio a due Mandolini e Basso (1789)	Noseda M 24.9	
Giuliano, G.	Sonata di Mandolino Solo è Basso	Noseda M 15.12	
Giuliano, G.	[6] Duetti	Noseda M 15.13	
Giuliano, G.	[4] Duetti per Mandolini	Noseda M 15.14	
Giuliano, G.	Mandolino Primo	Noseda M 15.15	For 2 mandes.
Giuliano, G.	Duetto a due Mandolini	Noseda M 15.16	
Giuliano, G.	Duetto à due Mandolini	Noseda M 15.17	
Giuliano, G.	Duetto a due Mandolini	Noseda M 15.18	
Giuliano, G.	Duetto a due Mandolini	Noseda M 15.19	
Giuliano, G.	Duetto a due Mandolini	Noseda M 15.20	
Giuliano, G.	Duetto A due Mandolini	Noseda M 15.21	
Giuliano, G.	Basso. Trio Notturno a due Mandolini e Basso	Noseda M 15.22	
Guerra, A.	Sonata a Mandolino solo e Basso	Noseda M 28.4	
Lauro, G.	Duetto a due Mandolini (1789)	Noseda L 18.18	
Lauro, G.	Sonata Per Mandolino Solo e Basso	Noseda L 18.19	
Leoné	Duetto a due Mandolini (1789)	Noseda O 30.37	A copy of Leoné's 'Duo IV' (Paris, 1762)
Leoné	Duetto a due Mandolini (1789)	Noseda O 30.38	A copy of Leoné's 'Duo III' (Paris, 1762)
Leoné	Sonata per due Mandolini	Noseda O 30.39	A copy of Leoné's 'Duo V' (Paris, 1762)
Leoné	Trio a due Mandolini, e Basso	Noseda O 30.40	
Rava, G.	Duetto a due Mandolini	Noseda P 30.6	
Terreni, B.	Minuetto	Noseda P 34.13	For amandolino and cembalo
Terreni, B.	Sonata	Noseda P 34.14	mande and basso

Location: I:MTventuri

Anon.	Duo per mandolino e violino	A 279	
Anon.	6 sonate per 2 mandolini [in G, D, A, F, G, D]	A 201	
Anon.	6 sonate per 2 mandolini [in F, F, C, F, B, D]	A 280	
Andreozzi, G.	Aria con mandolino e archiliuto obbl. 'Frena col pianto o cava	A 182	
Bianciardi	Sonate per 1 ò 2 mandoli	A 169	
Cappelletti, C.	Sonate per 1 ò 2 mandolini	A 169	
Giuliani, G. F.	Sonate per 1 ò 2 mandolini	A 169	

COMPOSER	TITLE	SHELF NO	REMARKS
Giuliani, G. F.	Quartetto quinto	A 111	For mande., fl. or vn., va., and vc. Incomplete
Giuliani, G. F.	Sonata per mandolinio solo e Basso	A 112	
Macia, I.	Trio per flauto e 2 mandolini	A 141	
Moneta, G.	Sonate per 1 ò 2 mandolini	A 169	
Paisiello, G.	Cavatina con mandolino obbligato 'Saper bramare'	A 146	
Panerai, V.	Suonata per cembalo, mandolino ò violino	A 168	A copy of the published edition in I:PS
Sforgi, A.	6 duetti per 2 mandolini	A 142	
Sforgi, A.	7 sonate per mandolino e basso	A 143	
Sforgi, A.	Sonate per 1 ò 2 mandolini	A 169	

Location: I:Nc

Barbella, E.	Duetto Per Due Mandolini	22. 2. 15 MS. 182/5	
Paisiello, G.	[Aria from *The Barber of Seville*]		

Location: I:Ps

Gambini, G.	Trio per due Mandolini e basso	B. 203/6	

Location: I:Rv

Giuliani, G. F.	6 Notturni per 2 mandolini e basso	161	

Location: S:Skma

Giuliani, G.	Sonata in E♯ — C — Per Mandolino, e Basso	B 15	3-movt. sonata in E
Giuliani, G.	Sonata in Es♮ — C — Per Mandolino, e Basso	B 16	3-movt. sonata in E♭

Location: S:Uu[6]

Barbella, E.	Sonata a Due mandolinj	Gimo 12	
Barbella, E.	Duetto a due Mandolinj	Gimo 13	
Barbella, E.	Sonata a Due Mandolini	Gimo 14	

[6] These MSS date from the early 1760s.

COMPOSER	TITLE	SHELF NO	REMARKS
Barbella, E.	Sonata à Due Mandolinj	Gimo 15, 16, 17	Multiple copies
Barbella, E.	Sonata a due Mandolini e Basso	Gimo 18, 19	Multiple copies
Cecere, C.	Concerto Di Mandolino con Violini, e Basso (1762)	Gimo 60	For 2 vns. and basso
Cocchi, G.	Sinfonia a due Mandolini, e Basso	Gimo 76	
Gabellone, G.	Concerto Di Mandolino con Violini e Basso Obligati	Gimo 88	For 2 vns. and basso
Gaudioso, D.	Concerto di mandolino a solo con Violini e Basso	Gimo 58	For 2 vns. and basso
Gervasio, G. B.	Sonata a Mandolino Solo e Basso	Gimo 141	
Gervasio, G. B.	Sonata per Camera di Mandolino, e Basso (1762)	Gimo 142, 143	Multiple copies
Gervasio, G. B.	Sonata per Camera di Mand:no è Basso	Gimo 144	
Gervasio, G. B.	Sonata Per Camera Di Mandolino, e Basso	Gimo 145, 146	Multiple copies
Gervasio, G. B.	Duetto a due Mandolini	Gimo 147, 148	Multiple copies
Gervasio, G. B.	Sinfonia a due mannolinj, è Basso	Gimo 149	
Gervasio, G. B.	Trio a Due Mandolini e Basso	Gimo 150	
Giuliano, G.	Sinfoni per Mannolino con Più Istromenti	Gimo 153	For 2 vns. and basso
Ugolino, V.	Basso Concerto Per Mandolino Violino Primo Violino Secondo e Basso	Gimo 297	
Anon.	Trio a Due Mandolinj e Basso	Gimo 359	

Appendix IV

Music Examples

1 *Suonata Decimquarto per Cimbalo a pianoforte e Mandolino o Violino obbligato* by Vincenzo Panerai: this is one of the few eighteenth-century compositions for mandoline with a fully written-out keyboard part. The upper stave of the keyboard occupies the same tessitura as the mandoline, rather than simply accompanying it in a lower register, and great use is made throughout of imitation.

2 *Six Sonates pour la Mandoline avec la Basse*, Op. 2, by Leoné: the bass line of this piece seems to be intended for cello, as it can all be played on the G string, *la terza corda*. The upper part is typical of Leoné's florid, highly ornamented style of mandoline writing.

Suonata Decimquarto per Cimbalo a pianoforte e Mandolino o Violino obbligato (Florence, *c.*1780), by Vincenzo Panerai. 1st movt.

Source: I:PS B. 199 n. 6

Six Sonates pour la Mandoline avec la Basse, Op. 2 (Paris, 1777), by Leoné. Sonata II, 2nd movt.

Source: GB:Lbl

Bibliography

ABBOTT, D., and SEGERMAN, E. (1976). 'Gut Strings', *Early Music*, 4/4.

AGAZZARI, AGOSTINO (1607). *Del sonare sopra'l basso con tutti li stromenti e dell'uso loro nel conserto* (Siena; repr. Bologna, 1969).

AGRICOLA, MARTIN (1529). *Musica instrumentalis deudsch* (Wittenberg; enlarged 5th edn., 1545; repr. Leipzig, 1969).

ALBRECHTSBERGER, JOHANN GEORG (1790). *Anweisung zur Composition* (Vienna).

AMAT, JOAN CARLOS (*c*.1703–13). *Guitarra espanola* (Gerona); including the anonymous 'Tractat breu'.

ASTON, JOHN (1882). *Social Life in the Reign of Queen Anne* (London).

BACH, CARL PHILIPP EMANUEL (1759). *Versuch über die wahre Art das Clavier zu spielen* (Berlin).

BAINES, ANTHONY (1966). *European and American Musical Instruments* (New York).

BARLOW, JEREMY, ed. (1985). *The Complete Country Dance Tunes from Playford's Dancing Master (1651–c.1728)* (London).

BECHERINI, BIANCA (1959). *Catalogo dei Manoscritti Musicali della Biblioteca Nazionale di Firenze* (Kassel).

BERMUDO, JUAN (1555). *Libro primo de la declaracion de instrumentos* (Ossuna; 1st edn., 1549; repr. 1957).

BOETTICHER, WOLFGANG (1978). *Lauten-und Gittarrentabulaturen de 15. bis 18. Jahrhunderts*, Répertoire international des sources musicales (Kassel).

BONANI, FILIP (1722). *Gabinetto armonico* (Rome).

BORTOLAZZI, BARTHOLOMEO (1805). *Anweisung die Mandoline* (Leipzig).

BOWMAN, ROBIN (1981). 'Musical Information in the Archives of the Church of S. Maria Maggiore, Bergamo, 1649–1720', in Ian Bent (ed.), *Source Materials and the Interpretation of Music.* (London).

BROOK, BARRY S., ed. (1966). *The Breitkopf Thematic Catalogue 1762–1787* (New York).

BROWN, HOWARD MAYER (1965). *Instrumental Music Printed Before 1600: A Bibliography* (Cambridge, Mass.).

——(1973). *Sixteenth Century Instrumentation* (Rome).

BRUNET, PIERRE (1578). *Tablature de Mandorre* (Paris; lost).

BURNEY, CHARLES (1771). *An Eighteenth Century Musical Tour in France and Italy*, 2 vols. (London).

CAMPBELL, RICHARD (1980). 'Mandolin' in *New Grove Dictionary of Music and Musicians* (London).

CASTELLANI, MARCELLO (1985). *Gaetano Boni: Divertimenti per camera* (Intro. to facs. edn., Florence).

CHITZ, A., (1912). 'Une œuvre inconnue de Beethoven pour mandoline et piano', *Sammelbünde der Internationalen Musikgesellschaft. Revue musicale*, 8/12.

CHORON, ALEXANDER ÉTIENNE, and FAYOLLE, F. J. M. (1810). *Dictionnaire historique de musiciens* (Paris).

COATES, KEVIN (1985). *Geometry, Proportion and the Art of Lutherie* (London).

—— (1977). 'The Mandoline, an Unsung Serenader', *Early Music*, 5/1.

COGGIN, PHILIP (1987). ' "This Easy and Agreable Instrument", A History of the English Guittar', *Early Music*, 15: 205–18.

CORRETTE, MICHEL (1772). *Nouvelle Méthode pour apprendre à Jouer en très peu de tems de la Madôline [sic]* (Paris; repr. Geneva, 1985).

COVARRUBIAS, SEBASTIAN DE (1611). *Tesoro de la lingua castellana* (Madrid).

CRISTOFORETTI, ORLANDO, ed. (1984). *Dalla Casa Manuscript* (Intro. to facs. edn., Florence).

—— (1982). *G. Zamboni: Sonate . . . 1718* (Intro. to facs. edn., Florence).

CROOKS, DAVID Z., trans. and ed. (1987). *Michael Praetorius: Syntagma Musicum II De Organographia, Parts I and II* (London).

DAVIDSSON, A. K. E. (1963). *Catalogue of the Gimo Collection of Italian Manuscript Music in the University Library of Uppsala* (Uppsala).

DENIS, PIETRO (1768, pt 1; 1769, pt 2; 1773, pt 3). *Méthode Pour Apprendre à Jouer de la Mandoline* (Paris; repr. Geneva, 1984).

DIDEROT, DENIS, ed. (1751–76). *Encyclopédie* (Paris).

DONINGTON, ROBERT (1980). 'Ornaments' in *New Grove Dictionary of Music and Musicians* (London).

DOWNING, J. (1981). 'An Inventory of the Charles van Raalte Collection of Instruments', *Fellowship of Makers and Restorers of Historical Instruments [FOMRHI] Quarterly* 24.

DRUMMOND, PIPPA (1980). *The German Concerto* (London).

DUCHARTRE, PIERRE LOUIS (1929). *The Italian Comedy* (London; repr. New York, 1966).

ELKIN, ROBERT (1955). *The Old Concert Rooms of London* (London).

FÉTIS, FRANCOIS JOSEPH (1873). *Biographie Universelle des Musiciens* (Paris.)

FISKE, ROGER (1973). *English Theatre Music in the Eighteenth Century* (London; 2nd end., Oxford, 1986).

FOUCHETTI, GIOVANNI (1771). *Méthode pour apprendre facilement à jouer de la Mandoline à 4 et à 6 Cordes* (Paris; repr. Geneva, 1984).

FRISOLI, P. (1971). 'The Museo Stradivariano in Cremona', *Galpin Society Journal*, 24.

GAMBASSI, O. (1984). 'Origine, statuti e ordinamenti del Concerto Palatino della Signoria di Bologna (III)', *Nuova rivista musicale italiana*, 4.

GASPARI, GAETANO (1893). *Catalogo della Biblioteca del Liceo Musicale di Bologna*, 3 (Bologna; repr, 1961).

GASPARI, GAETANO, and GALLO, F. (1918–34). *Catalogo delle opere musicali; Città di Napoli*, 10 (Parma).

GERBER, ERNEST LUDWIG (1790). *Historisch-Biographisches Lexicon der Tonkünstler* (Leipzig).

—— (1812–14). *Neues Historisch-Biographisches Lexicon der Tonkünstler* (Leipzig; repr. 1966).

GERVASIO, GIOVANNI BATTISTA (1767). *Méthode très facile Pour apprendre à jouer de la Mandoline à quatre Cordes Instrument fait pour les Dames* (Paris).

GILL, DONALD (1984). 'Mandolin' in *New Grove Dictionary of Musical Instruments* (London).

—— (1984). 'Colascione' in *New Grove Dictionary of Musical Instruments* (London).

GLADD, NEIL (1987). 'The Classical Mandolin in America' in *Classical Mandolin Society of America*, 1/4: 7–11.

GODWIN, J. (1973). 'The Survival of the Theorbo Principle', *Journal of the Lute Society of America*, 6: 4–17.

GOUIRAND, ANDRÉ (1908). *La Musique en Provence et le Conservatoire de Marseille* (Marseilles).

HAMBLY, SCOTT (1977). 'Mandolins in the U.S. since 1880' (Doct. diss., University of Pennsylvania).

HAMMOND, F. (1974). 'Musicians at the Medici Court in the Mid-Seventeenth Century', *Analecta musicologica*, 14.

—— (1979). 'Girolamo Frescobaldi and a Decade of Music in Casa Barberini', *Analecta musicologica*, 19.

HARWOOD, IAN (1984). 'Tieffenbrucker' in *New Grove Dictionary of Musical Instruments* (London).

HELLWIG, F. (1974). 'Lute-making in the Late 15th and 16th Century', *Lute Society Journal*, 16.

HESS, W. (1948). 'Beethoven und die Mandoline', *Schweizeriche Musikzeitung*, Nov., 421–2.

—— (1952, trans.). 'Beethoven e il Mandolino', *La rassegna musicale*, 4: 317–20.

HIGHFILL, PHILIP, Jr. (1978). *A Biographical Dictionary of Actors, Actresses, Musicians, Dancers, Managers, and other Stage Personnel in London 1660–1800* (Carbondale).

HILL, GEORGE, FRANCIS (1930). *A Corpus of Italian Medals of the Renaissance* (London).

HIPKINS, ALFRED JAMES (1954). 'String' in *Grove Dictionary of Music and Musicians* (London).

JEZE, [?] (1759). *Tableau de Paris* (Paris).

JOHANSSON, CARI (1955). *French Music Publishers' Catalogues of the Second Half of the Eighteenth Century* (Stockholm).

KASTNER, JEAN GEORGES (1837). *Traité général d'instrumentation* (Paris).

LEONÉ, [?]. (1768). *Méthode Raisonnée Pour Passer du Violon à la Mandoline* (Paris; repr. of 1768 edn.: Geneva, 1984). English trans., *A complete introduction to the art of playing the mandoline* (London, 1785).

LE ROUX, DIDIER (1986). 'La Mandoline aux "Concerts Spirituels" Parisiens du XVIIIme siècle', *Journal de la pratique musicale des amateurs*, 396: 10–14.

LE ROY, ADRIAN (1585). *L'Instruction pour la mandorre* (Paris; lost).

LESURE, FRANÇOIS, ed. (1981). *Catalogue de la musique imprimée avant 1800 conservée dans les bibliothèques publiques de Paris* (Paris).

LESURE, FRANÇOIS and THIBAULT, G. (1966). 'La Méthode de mandoline de Michel Corrette', *Fontes Artes Musicae*, 1.

LIESS, A. (1957). 'Materialien zür römischen Musikgeschichte des Seicento', *Acta musicologica*, 29.

LIGASACCHI, G. (1985). 'Bartolomeo Bortolazzi, Virtuoso di Mandolino e Compositore', *1^a Rassegna Nazionale di Strumenti a Pizzico, Brescia*.

LITCHFIELD, R. B. (1981). 'Naples under the Bourbons', in *The Golden Age of Naples—Art and Civilisation Under the Bourbons 1734–1805* (Detroit Institute of Arts, Chicago).

LOCKWOOD, L. (1975). 'Pietrobono and the Instrumental Tradition in Ferrara in the Fifteenth Century', *Rivista italiana di musicologia*, 10.

LÜTGENDORFF, WILLIBALD LEO VON (1922). *Die Geigen und Lautenmacher vom Mittalter bis zur Gegenwart* (Frankfurt-am-Main).

LUYNES, DUC DE (1860). *Mémoires* (extracts rep. Paris 1970, ed. Norbert Dufourcq).

MAGGINI, EMILIO, ed. (1965). *Catalogo del Fondo Musicale nella Biblioteca del Seminario di Lucca* (*Bibliotheca Musicae, 3*) (Milan).

MANN, WILLIAM (1977). *The Operas of Mozart* (London).

MARX, H. J. (1968). 'Die Musik am Hofe Kardinal Ottoboni's unter Arcangelo Corelli', *Analecta musicologica*, 5.

—— (1983). 'Die "Giustificazioni della Casa Pamphili" als Musikgeschichtliche Quelle', *Studi musicali*, 12.

MEE, JOHN H. (1911). *The Oldest Music Room in Europe* (London).

MERSENNE, MARIN (1636). *Harmonie universelle* (Paris; repr. 1963).

MEYLAN, R. (1958). 'Collection Antonio Venturi', *Fontes artes musicae*, 5: 31.

MILLIOT, SYLVETTE (1970). *Documents inédits sur les luthiers Parisiens du XVIIIme siècle* (Paris).

MINGUET Y YROL, PABLO (*c*.1752). *Reglas, y advertencias generales para tañer la bandurria* (Madrid; repr. Geneva, 1984).

—— (*c*.1752). *Reglas, y advertencias generales para tañer la guitarra, tiple, y vandola* (Madrid; repr. Geneva, 1984).

MOOSER, R. ALOYS (1948–51). *Annales de la musique et les musiciens en Russie au XVIIIme siècle* (Geneva).

MOTTA, TOMASSO (1681). *Armonica capricciosa di suonate musicali* (Milan).

NEUMANN, FREDERICK (1978). *Ornamentation in Baroque and Post-Baroque Music* (Princeton).

NICOLL, ALLARDYCE (1963). *The World of Harlequin* (Cambridge).

PAGE, CHRISTOPHER (1980). 'Fourteenth-Century Instruments and Tunings: A Treatise by Jean Vaillant? (Berkeley, Ms. 744)', *Galpin Society Journal*, 33.

PANDOLFI, VITO (1957). *La Commedia Dell'Arte* (Florence).

PARISINI, F., and COLOMBANI, E. (1881). *Catalogo dell collezione d'autografi lasciata alla R. Accademia Filarmonica di Bologna* (Bologna).

PEGGE, SAMUEL (1796). *Anonymania* (London).

PICCININI, ALESSANDRO (1623). *Intavolatura di liuto, et di chitarrone, libro primo* (Bologna; repr. 1962).

PIERRE, CONSTANT (1975). *Histoire du Concert Spirituel 1725–90* (Paris).

PINTACUDA, SALVATORE, ed. (1966). *Catalogo del Fondo Antico nella Biblioteca dell'Istituto Musicale 'N. Paganini' di Genova* (*Bibliotheca Musicae, 4*) (Milan).

PISANI, AGOSTINO (1913). *Manuale teorico pratico del mandolinista* (Milan).

PITRELLI, A. (*c*.1983). 'Il mandolino nella musica del secolo XVIII', *Notiziario dell'Accademia Chitarra Classica*, 37.

PLAYFORD, JOHN (1652). *A Booke of New Lessons for Cithern and Gittern* (London).

POHLMANN, ERNST (1975, 4th edn.). *Laute, Theorbe, Chitarrone* (Bremen; 5th edn., 1982).

PRAETORIUS, MICHAEL (1618–19). *Syntagma Musicum* (*tomus secundus*) (Wolfenbüttel; repr. Kassel, 1958).

—— (1620). *Theatrum instrumentorum* (Wolfenbüttel; repr. Kassel, 1958).

PREFUMO, D. (1978*a*). 'I manoscritti mandolistici Genovesi', *Notiziario dell' Accademia Chitarra Classica*, 32.

—— (1978*b*). 'Musiche sconosciute e poco note con chitarra e mandolino di Alessandro Rolla', *Notiziario dell'Accademia Chitarra Classica*, 32.

—— (1979). 'Paganini e il Mandolino', *Notiziario dell'Accademia Chitarra Classica*, 33.

RICCI, GIOVANNI PIETRO (1677). *Scuola d'intavolatura . . .* (Rome).

ROSCI, MARCO (1971). *Baschenis, Bettera & Co. Produzione e Mercata della Natura Morta del Seicento in Italia* (Milan).

ROUSSEAU, JEAN-JACQUES (1753). *Lettre sur la musique française* (Paris).

RYOM, PETER (1986). *Répertoire des œuvres d'Antonio Vivaldi: Les Compositions Instrumentales* (Copenhagen).

SACCONI, SIMONE, F. (1979). *The 'Secrets' of Stradivari* (Cremona).

SACHS, CURT (1913). *Real-lexicon* (Berlin).

SAFFLE, M. (1976). 'Lutes and Related Instruments in Eight Important European and American Collections', *Journal of the Lute Society of America*, 9.

SAINSBURY, JOHN (1825). *A Dictionary of Musicians.* (London).

SAINT-FOIX, GEORGES DE (1933). 'Un fonds inconnu de compositions pour mandoline (XVIIIme siècle)', *Revue de musicologie*, 14: 129–35.

SARTORI, CLAUDIO (1952). *Bibliografia della musica strumentale italiana*, 1 (Florence).

—— (1962). *Catalogo del Fondo Musicale nella Biblioteca Comunale di Assisi (Bibliotheca Musicae, 1)* (Milan).

SCHEURLEER, D. F. (1893). *Catalogue der Musiekbibliotheek* (The Hague).

SCHLOSSER, JULIUS VON (1920). *Die Sammlung alter Musikinstrumente* (Vienna; repr. 1974).

SEGERMAN, E. (1986). 'Neapolitan mandolins, wire strengths and violin stringing in late 18th century France', *FORMHI Quarterly*, 43.

SILBIGER, ALEXANDER (1980). *Italian Manuscript Sources of 17th Century Keyboard Music* (Ann Arbor).

SMITH, D. A. (1980). 'Sylvius Leopold Weiss', *Early Music*, 8/1.

SMOLLETT, TOBIAS (1766). *Travels through France and Italy* (London).

SOTOS, ANDRÉS DE (1764). *Arte para aprender . . . la guitarra* (Madrid).

SPALDING CLUB, THE (1848). *A Genealogical Deduction of the Family of Rose of Kilravock* (Edinburgh).

SPENCER, ROBERT (1976). 'The Chitarrone Francese', *Early Music*, 4: 164–6.

SPENCER ROBERT, and HARWOOD, IAN (1984). 'English Guitar' in *New Grove Dictionary of Musical Instruments* (London).

STRUNK, O. (1952). *Source Readings in Music History* (London).

TALBOT, MICHAEL (1984). *Vivaldi* (London).

TYLER, JAMES (1975). 'The Renaissance Guitar 1500–1650', *Early Music*, 3/4.

—— (1980). *The Early Guitar* (London).

—— (1981a). 'The Mandore in the 16th and 17th Centuries', *Early Music*, 9/1: 22–31.

—— (1981b). 'The Italian Mandolin and Mandola 1589–1800', *Early Music*, 9/4: 438–46.

—— ed., (1983). *Gasparo Zanetti: Il Scolaro (1645)*, 2 vols. (London).

—— (1984). 'Guitar' in *New Grove Dictionary of Musical Instruments* (London).

VALLAS, LÉON (1908). *La musique à l'Académie de Lyon au dix-huitième siècle* (Lyon).

—— (1932). *Un siècle de musique et de théâtre à Lyon 1688–1789* (Lyon).

VANNES, RENÉ (1951). *Dictionnaire universel des luthiers* (Brussels; repr. 1975).

VIRDUNG, SEBASTIAN (1511). Musica getutscht (Basle; repr. Kassel, 1970).

WEAVER, ROBERT L., and NORA W. (1978). *A Chronology of Music in the Florentine Theater 1590–1750* (Detroit).

WESSELY-KROPIK, HELENE (1961). *Lelio Colista, ein römischer Meister vor Corelli* (Vienna).

WHISTLING, CARL FRIEDRICH, and HOFMEISTER, FRIEDRICH (1817–27). *Handbuch der Musikalischen Litteratur* (repr. New York, 1975).

WINTERNITZ, EMANUEL (1966). *Die schönsten Musikinstrumente des Abendlandes* (Munich).

WITHERELL, ANNE L. (1983). *Louis Pecour's 1770 Recueil de dances* (Ann Arbor).

WOLF, JOHANNES (1919). *Handbuch der Notationskunde* (Leipzig; repr. Hildesheim, 1963).

WÖLKI, KONRAD (1939). *Geschichte der Mandoline* (Berlin); trans. by Keith Harris (Arlington VA, 1984) as *History of the Mandolin*.

WRIGHT, L. (1977). 'The Medieval Gittern and Citole: A Case of Mistaken Identity', *Galpin Society Journal*, 30.

—— (1984). 'Gittern' in *New Grove Dictionary of Musical Instruments* (London).

ZUTH, JOSEF (1926). *Handbuch der Laute und Gitarre* (Vienna; repr. Hildesheim, 1972).

—— (1931). 'Die Mandolinehandschriften in der Bibliothek der Gesellschaft der Musikfreunde in Wien', *Zeitschrift für Musikwissenschaft*, 19.

Periodicals Consulted

Affiches de Lyon (Lyon, 1759–72)

Allgemeine musikalische Zeitung (Leipzig, 1798–1848)

Almanach de Lyon (Lyon, 1756, 1761)

Almanach musical (Paris, 1775–83)

Annonces, affiches et avis divers (Paris, 1760–72)

l'Avant-coureur des spectacles (Paris, c.1760–80)

Avis divers (Paris, c.1760–91)

Calendrier Musical Universel (Paris, 1788–9)

Grove Dictionary of Music and Musicians (5th edn., London, 1954)

Journal de Musique (Paris, 1770–7; facs. repr. by Minkoff Reprint, Geneva)

Journal de Paris (Paris, 1783)
Mercure de France (Paris, 1749–85)
New Grove Dictionary of Music and Musicians (London, 1980)
New Grove Dictionary of Musical Instruments (London, 1984)
Tablettes de renommée des musiciens (Paris, 1785)

Index

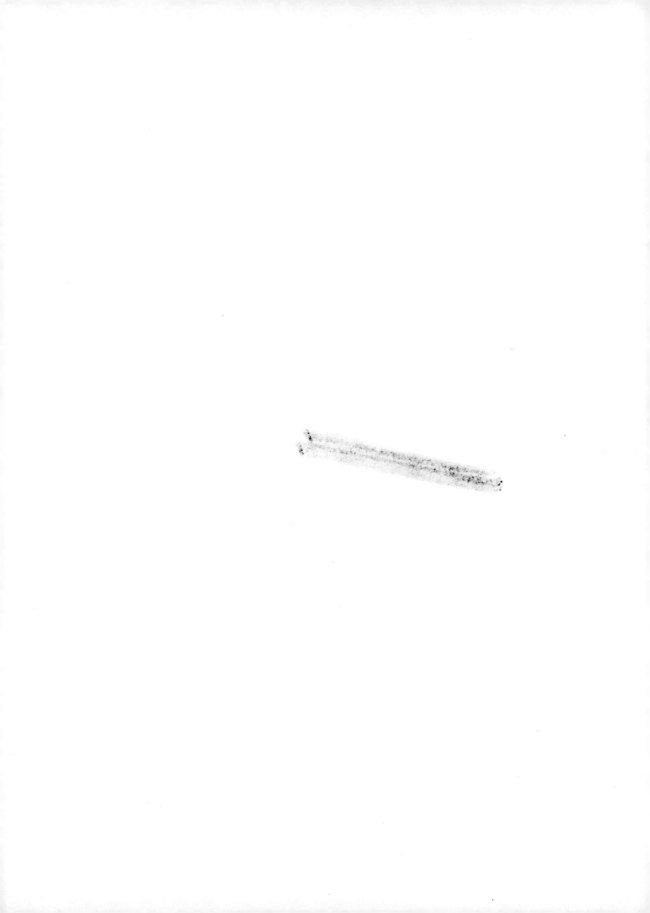